Women of Royalty
Revealing God's Plan
for His Daughters

Shirley Sustar

Treasure House

An Imprint of
Destiny Image® **Publishers, Inc.**
P.O. Box 310
Shippensburg, PA 17257-0310

ISBN 1-56043-314-0

For Worldwide Distribution
Printed in the U.S.A.

This book and all other Destiny Image, Revival Press,
and Treasure House books are available
at Christian bookstores and distributors worldwide.

For a U.S. bookstore nearest you, call **1-800-722-6774**.
For more information on foreign distributors, call **717-532-3040**.
Or reach us on the Internet: **http://www.reapernet.com**

Dedication

This book is dedicated to women of every race and age. May you come to know and experience the fullness of God's love and purpose for your life.

Acknowledgments

I wish to express my gratitude to all those who helped make *Women of Royalty* possible.

First and foremost to my Daddy-God who brought revelation and light to my life, and put His word in my heart and in my mouth.

To my husband Jim for his confidence in me and in the Spirit that dwells within me; who always blesses and encourages the work of my hands.

To my children, sisters, parents, parents-in-law, and church family for their prayers and encouragement.

To Bill Beery, our associate pastor, for his prophetic encouragement and support.

To Teri Beery, Carol Buchwalter, Tiffany Buchwalter, Deb Grande, Karen Noe, Debbie Snyder, Sandy Sustar, Joe and Sheryl Villegas, and Bev Wade for critiquing the original manuscript and/or serving me in practical ways.

To Dennis Cramer, Melinda Fish, Jan Garber, Michal Ann Goll, Ron and Lily King, and John Watson for their encouragement and endorsement.

And finally, to Elizabeth Allen, Laura Greenlee, Marsha Blessing, Philip Zook, and the entire staff at Destiny Image.

Endorsements

"True authentic Christianity is to love the Lord with all your heart. This book captures the heart of Abba Father. We have had the privilege of knowing Shirley Sustar, the author of this book, for many years and can say that she lives and exemplifies the Father's love in her life. We highly recommend *Women of Royalty* to God's daughters and sons."

Ron King, Director
Apostolic Team Ministries Intl.
Lily King, Director
Apostolic Team Ministries Intl. Women's Council

"...simply the best book on the heart of God I've ever read. One cannot go away unchanged after reading *Women of Royalty*. I suspect Shirley Sustar may have a classic on her hands."

Dennis Cramer, Prophet and Author

"*Women of Royalty* is a message of utmost importance to Christian women today. I believe that God's anointing will rest upon this book and minister to every person who reads it."

Dr. Jan L. Garber, President
Vision Christian Bible College

"Shirley Sustar's *Women of Royalty* opens your heart to the Father's healing love. Through honest testimony and in-depth insight she unfolds God's plan for you in hard times. This book is a tool in God's hand to help prepare women to emerge from difficulty with a passion for Jesus to take their places as effective leaders in His Kingdom. It will change any heart that's open."

Melinda Fish, Author and Co-Pastor,
Church of the Risen Savior

"As I read this book, I could see and hear the author speaking. I have known Shirley for several years and she is a living manifestation of her book. This book is excellent material to use as a devotional guide. By applying this fine material the lady of God will arise in real maturity. I eager-ly recommend this book and the author to God-fearers and God-seekers."

John Watson, Senior Pastor and Apostle
Marion Christian Center

Contents

Foreword

Introduction

Chapter 1   The King Is Daddy! 1

Chapter 2   Relating to Daddy-God 11

Chapter 3   A Spirit of Excellence! 23

Chapter 4   "Tell My Daughters..." 35

Chapter 5   Preparing Ourselves to Be Presented 45

Chapter 6   Recognizable Beauty 57

Chapter 7   The Big Lie! 75

Chapter 8   "I've Chosen You—Come Forth!" 89

Chapter 9   Get Ready... Get Set... Go! 105

Chapter 10   Women of Authority and Power 123

Foreword

I once had a vision of a wedding ceremony. Hundreds of guests stood in honor of the bride who was about to make her way down the aisle to her waiting groom. She was dressed in a beautiful white gown, and delicate white lace veiled her face. She was lovely in form and face. Her groom, standing at the altar, eagerly anticipated her presence by his side. Everything he held in his heart for his beloved could be clearly seen just by looking into his eyes. He seemed to desire for her eyes to lock with his; he wanted to show her his undying love and faithfulness through his gaze. He wanted their gazes to meet and never be broken apart. But, as the bride approached, she could not bring herself to lift her eyes from the floor. Even though she was beautiful and totally desired by her groom, she felt unworthy of the match, and shame covered her heart. If she only could have found the courage to look into her groom's eyes, she would have found all the love she would have ever needed to erase every trace of shame and unworthiness from her heart and mind.

I believe that the Lord is releasing His ardent gaze of love toward His daughters in a fresh and powerful way! He is out to win us and woo us. All He is asking us to do is just to "look into My eyes and tell Me what you see!" He is revealing Himself to us, His Loveliness, His Faithfulness, and He is so gently and graciously healing old wounds and scars of fear and torment.

Love is the key because "...perfect love turns fear out of doors and expels every trace of terror" (1 Jn. 4:18a AMP). In order to become the kind of Bride that we are destined to be, all our fears and feelings of unworthiness *must* be reduced to nothing. The Bride of Christ is to become like Esther, requiring only those things that Hegai the king's attendant, the keeper of the women, suggested (see Esth. 2:15).

We would be wise to look at Hegai as being representative of the Holy Spirit and apply that same principle to our lives. Our lifelong act of love and devotion to our King should be to choose only those things that the Holy Spirit deems pleasing to our heavenly Father, the King of kings. In so doing, we will enter into the favor of the Lord and experience deep intimacy with Him.

We, as the Bride of Christ, are to boldly and confidently come into the throne room and touch the scepter of the Lord that has been extended to us. We are to rule with Jesus, not in haughtiness, but in true humility and service. Because He first loved us, He opened the way so that we could love Him and be with Him throughout eternity.

The wedding ceremony is at hand, and we are dressed in bridal adornment. As we come down the aisle, will we look into the Bridegroom's eyes and be forever transformed by what we see there? We must take courage! We must look up, and enter into our destiny to become *"women of royalty"*!

With these thoughts, I recommend to you this book written by Shirley Sustar. I have found her to be a woman devoted to God, grounded in His Word, and hungry to give away to others what she herself has received from her Father. I have found this book to be a great encouragement to press in to know my Daddy-God as He truly is!

Michal Ann Goll
Antioch, Tennessee

Introduction

I have been married for 31 years to Jim Sustar, senior pastor of Heartland Christian Center where I actively serve alongside my husband. I have four children ranging from ages 12 to 27 years of age. The first two are now married.

Along with ministering outside our local congregation, in the United States and abroad, I lead the women's ministry at Heartland Christian Center in training teams of women to teach, counsel, and help give oversight to other women. I serve on the Women's Counsel for Apostolic Team Ministries, based in Toledo, Ohio, in association with the network of churches with which Heartland is affiliated. I also direct the post-abortion support group and Bible study at the Pregnancy Care Center of Wayne County. I have a love for the prophetic and a passion to see women recognize their potential in Christ Jesus.

Women of Royalty is a book that recognizes that God's daughters, having been purchased by the costly blood of God's dear Son, have a destiny and purpose to fulfill. Women all over the earth feel bound by wounds of the past and present, and these wounds, along with feelings of inferiority and insecurity, keep them from recognizing their potential and purpose in Christ Jesus.

This book is written for women of all ages. It is unique in the fact that it not only points out emotions and feelings that many women can relate to, but it also uncovers a mentality that produces attitudes and behaviors that are keeping women all over the earth in bondage and unhappiness.

Psalm 45:9 (AMP) says, "Kings' daughters are among Your honorable women...." My hope and prayer is that this book will cause women to find their dignity and identity in God and help to bring them to a place of emotional and spiritual maturity. I am convinced that as Christian women recognize who they are and how God has provided for them to get to where they're going, they will become free to display their Father's attributes and character along with God's glorious love and grace.

My own testimony demonstrates the importance of this revelation. For I have known about God and been surrounded by Christians for as long as I can remember. I was born into a Christian family that sought God's will and direction in all that they did. We prayed in the mornings, throughout the day, before meals, and at bedtime. Jesus was the head of our home, and I soon learned that He was and will always be the eternal King.

My parents taught me that I actually have two Fathers— my father on earth and my Father in Heaven. At a very young age, I began to develop a holy admiration and love for my heavenly Father, and at age eight, I received the Lord into my heart. I met my husband Jim and fell deeply in love with him when I was only 17 years old. He, too, had been brought up in a Christian home; his parents had been ministers since before he was born. We both had been taught that Christianity is a lifestyle, not merely a service or list of rules. The people we observed lived uncompromising lives. They loved God and had a passion to walk in purity and holiness.

By the late 1960s, however, the standard for righteous living seemed to be lowering, and it seemed that everywhere we looked, we saw Christians in compromise or upholding double standards in their attitudes and behavior. Looking back now, we recognize that we were young and were viewing these people through self-righteous eyes. We began to judge people rather than pray for them. We hadn't grown up in the Lord as we should have, so after being discouraged, disillusioned, and even wounded by some people, we pulled away from our local church. We intended to find another church somewhere, but somehow that just didn't happen. It didn't happen for four years!

Our eyes could only seem to see hypocrisy! Everywhere we looked, the scenario seemed the same. We never intended to walk away from God, nor did we ever say that we didn't want to serve the Lord anymore. Instead, we slowly became cold and indifferent ourselves, and before long we met new people and developed new friendships with people who were not Christians. We began to take on their ways of thinking and living, and we no longer thought about God's standards for our lives.

About four years later, we realized that we had fallen into a very serious backslidden state. The almighty dollar had become our god, and all our dreams were for material gain. By 6:30 a.m. each morning, Jim, along with the guys that he worked with, would begin drinking whiskey straight

•

from the bottle on the way to work. I never knew when he would come home at night, and I lived in constant fear.

Every night I went to bed fearing that I would die in my sleep or that my husband would be killed in a bar fight or from drunk driving. Thoughts of death became such a part of my life that a part of me was surprised every morning when I woke up to find that Jim and I were both still alive. My mental and emotional state was unhealthy to say the least, but because of the shameful way of life that we lived, I told no one. Our lives were completely undone. We hated the way we were living, yet we felt helpless to change it.

Although I had always wanted children, when I became pregnant during this time, I found myself begging God to take the child. I could not bear the thought of a precious little one growing up in our unhappy home.

There were times when my husband and I would discuss our spiritual state late at night. Because we knew that we were lost in sin and we feared the return of the Lord, we would agree to change our lifestyle and return to God. We knew how Christians were supposed to behave, so it never dawned on us that God would receive us just as we were and then change us. We were held captive by the enemy of our souls, the devil. We were ensnared and trapped by him, and we felt powerless to return to the Lord. So when the next day would dawn and our fear would lift, we would pretend we hadn't had our little talk the night before.

Four days before I gave birth to our daughter Jennifer, I began having what some people call false labor pains. These pains began while I was at a Christmas party with Jim, who was under the influence of alcohol. When I asked him to take me home, he became furious. He dropped me off and left me alone at the house. As he left, I called after him that if he still had the smell of alcohol on his breath when I was ready to deliver our baby that I would not allow him in the delivery room with me. I was terrified by my own words because I knew that would probably be the case and I didn't want to bring our child into the world by myself!

About 45 minutes later, my husband came back home with an apology and a pizza. I accepted his apology, but because I was feeling ill, I turned down the pizza. In my husband's still drunken state, this appeared to be a personal rejection. He became angry all over again, threw the pizza on the floor, lit up a cigarette, and poured himself another drink.

I began to cry. While still crying, I walked over to the television set and turned it on. Rex Humbard appeared, and he was preaching up a storm! He was throwing his arm toward the camera and pointing to the people in their homes saying things like, "You've been going to those bars!" (My husband told me later that every time Rex Humbard pointed, he felt like electricity was shooting through his body.) In only seconds, the anointing of God went through Rex Humbard and traveled almost 3,000 miles from Akron, Ohio, to Mont Claire, California. It came through our television set, hit my husband, and knocked him to the floor!

A tremendous battle took place within my husband's heart and mind that night in our living room. Satan was telling him that if he returned to God, he'd take everything from him. He'd take his wife, his child that was soon to be born, his job, his home...everything that he had! On the other hand, the Lord was saying, "If you return to Me, I *require* everything!" The Lord not only wanted Jim's life, but

He wanted Jim to give up his ownership of me, his child, job, home, and everything that he had. I got down on the floor with my husband, and both of us, broken and weeping together, returned to God in complete humility.

About an hour later, Jim and I arose from the floor. Jim was completely sober, and to this day—27 years later—he has not desired a drink. In fact, the very smell of alcohol makes him sick. The Lord delivered and transformed both of our lives. God took away my fear and filled us both with joy. Jim is now a pastor, and I'm convinced that he's the most wonderful man in the world!

What the Lord did for us was truly a miracle, but the greatest miracle that took place in us that day was the revelation that Jesus Christ is Lord and King. We had never had that understanding before. We had heard it said. We had even said it ourselves, but it had never become revelation to us until that moment. The new realization that Jesus is master, ruler, and in authority over all transformed and renewed our hearts and our minds.

The Bible tells us that God created everything. There isn't anything that is made that wasn't made by Him (see Jn. 1:3). He is the ruler of everything, and as I grew in the knowledge and understanding of the Lord, my heart also expanded in worship.

It is my desire for each woman who reads this book to receive a revelation of Jesus Christ as Savior, ruler, and master of all creation, and of God the Father as Daddy-God and the King who loves her and wants her to realize, experience, and fulfill all that He has purposed for her as a daughter of the King.

Chapter 1

The King Is Daddy!

Several years ago, I attended my first worship conference. While there I began to learn principles and truths about praise and worship that I had not previously experienced nor seen many churches put into practice. The leaders emphasized God's royal majesty through Scriptures like Psalm 24:7-10, which declares that the Lord is the King; Psalm 47:2, "...He is a great King over all the earth"; and Revelation 19:16, "...[He is] King of kings, and Lord of lords."

While we all fervently praised God, the leader's voice cried out, "The King is worthy of our praise! Sing a new song to the Lord!" The leader then instructed us to articulate what was in our hearts through a song to the Lord. With reverence and awe, I opened my mouth and began to sing words that declared His honor and majesty. Within seconds, I was lost in worship and caught up in an exciting vision.

Experience the Love and Pleasure of Daddy-God

In this vision, I suddenly moved from singing in worship to dancing before the King whom we were worshiping. I danced with all of my might, exuberantly leaping and spinning around and around in joyful praise! (I'm not a dancer in the natural, so this was not something I would ordinarily do. Since I've had this vision, I know that even though my ability to dance is something I'm sure others here on earth would prefer not to watch, in Heaven I'm going to be good!) In this vision, when I looked over my shoulder to see if I was staying in time with other dancers, panic gripped my heart! To my dismay, there wasn't anyone else in the room. Realizing my inadequacy and inability to entertain such a King, I almost stopped, but when I looked at His face, I could see that He was pleased. Not only was the King giving me His undivided attention, but He was leaning forward, smiling with an open, ear-to-ear grin! "Be-bopping" His head, the King joined in and kept time to the music by drumming His hands on the arms of the throne and tapping His feet.

I worshiped God with every fiber of my being, and as I did, there was a transfer of joy and enthusiasm between us. As I rejoiced in the Lord, He rejoiced over me. As I was enthralled by His presence, He was enthralled by my worship. I alone was responsible to entertain the King, and He was delighting in it. My worship intensified with wild abandonment right through the grand finale. (Now, since I'm not a dancer, this last part was quite impressive!) I ended the dance by doing a backward flip, landing in a split, and bowing before the King.

The King threw back His head in joyful laughter, while I jumped to my feet and ran to the throne. Suddenly, I was a small child again! As I reached the King, I hopped up on His lap. We laughed and hugged each other in sheer delight.

At that moment, I had a revelation like I never had before that the King is *Daddy*! The King of all ages, for all eternity, is my Daddy-God! While embracing God and sitting upon His lap, I giggled and laughed continuously. The joy and knowledge of God's goodness was intense. His great love made me feel completely accepted and set free. I knew I was safe and that everything would be all right as long as Daddy-God held me in His arms.

We cuddled and talked together, and as I leaned my head against His chest, I heard His heartbeat. I remember the awesome thrill I felt at the privilege to hear and feel such powerful Life. As I looked into His eyes, He communicated His love to me. Oh, what purity is in His eyes! What truth, love, and acceptance pours out from Daddy-God's eyes! Then, finally, I wrapped my arms around the King's neck, laid my head upon His shoulders, and rested.

Share the Knowledge of the King's Love

I remember thinking when the vision ended, *I can't wait to tell God's daughters!* For even though we might have the knowledge of God as our heavenly Father, many of us have not understood the intimacy He's called us to, nor what takes place through it. I've shared this vision of dancing before the King with women in different parts of the world, and many of these women have confessed that they long to experientially know a place of joy, intimacy, and security with God. Because so many women have been victimized and wounded by an earthly father (or by the lack of one), they have difficulty relating to God as their Daddy. Since intimacy requires us to make ourselves vulnerable, fear keeps these women at a distance from even their heavenly Father. However, the Word tells us that God made us and loves us with an everlasting love. He's not imperfect as earthly fathers are, and Daddy-God has only good gifts in store for His children. If we will draw near to the Father's heart and embrace Him, healing will come.

I believe God wants us to know that there is a purpose and a destiny for each one of His daughters to fulfill. However, before we can serve God's purposes, we must see and understand what they are. Then we must be given the ability to complete them. However, we must understand that the vision and strength necessary for fulfilling those purposes comes only through intimacy with God.

A short time after being given this vision, the Holy Spirit began dealing with me about it. He directed me to Romans chapter 8:

> *For as many as are led by the Spirit of God, they are the sons of God. For ye have not received the spirit of bondage again to fear; but ye have received the Spirit of adoption, whereby we cry, Abba, Father. The Spirit itself beareth witness with our spirit, that we are the children of God: and if children, then heirs; heirs of God, and joint-heirs with Christ; if so be that we suffer with Him, that we may be also glorified together* (Romans 8:14-16).

In this Epistle, Paul tells us that we have not been given a spirit of slavery that keeps us in bondage to fear, but we have received the spirit of adoption by which we cry, "Abba (Daddy), Father"! We have become God's very own children, and we share in the inheritance and glory with Christ. As daughters of the King, we also have a responsibility to demonstrate and to manifest the attributes of our Father. This means that our behavior should make who we are apparent to those around us. In other words, the fact that God is our Daddy should be obvious and plainly shown in our lives! The adage "like father, like daughter" should be true in each of our lives.

"In God's faithfullness lies eternal security."
Corrie Ten Boom

Because we have been made joint-heirs with Christ, we have the privilege of taking His name for ourselves, whereby, we can call ourselves Christians. Even though most of us

would never think of using God's name for cursing, when
we take God's name as our own and do not bear the responsibility of that name, we are truly taking it in vain!
Colossians 3:1-12 tells us that since we have been raised
with Christ, our minds should be set on the things that are
above and not on the earth. These verses instruct us to kill
the evil desires that try to control our lives, strip off the old
unregenerated self, and clothe ourselves as God's own chosen ones. That means we're to put on behavior belonging to
God! God calls us to live holy because He is holy.

> *[Live] as children of obedience [to God]; do not con-
> form yourselves to the evil desires [that governed
> you] in your former ignorance [when you did not
> know the requirements of the Gospel]. But as the One
> Who called you is holy, you yourselves also be holy
> in all your conduct and manner of living. For it is
> written, you shall be holy, for I am holy* (1 Peter
> 1:14-16 AMP).

God has saved us by His grace, purchased us with His
blood, and made us complete in Him. We cannot attain holiness through our own efforts and good works; it's only by
His grace that we're saved (see Eph. 2:5-9). However, we
can walk worthy of our calling in Christ Jesus by obeying
Hebrews 12:1-2.

> *Therefore then, since we are surrounded by so great
> a cloud of witnesses [who have borne testimony to
> the Truth], let us strip off and throw aside every en-
> cumbrance (unnecessary weight) and that sin which
> so readily (deftly and cleverly) clings to and entan-
> gles us, and let us run with patient endurance and
> steady and active persistence the appointed course of
> the race that is set before us, looking away [from all
> that will distract] to Jesus, Who is the Leader and
> Source of our faith [giving the first incentive for our*

belief] and is also its Finisher [bringing it to maturity and perfection]... (Hebrews 12:1-2 AMP).

By laying aside each and every encumbering sin, we choose to rid ourselves of worldly thinking and worldly ways. We must strip off those habitual sins that wrap themselves around our mind and emotions and keep us from moving forward in faith to maturity. If we don't, we will become bogged down and be unable to run the race to which God has called us. Each one of us has things in our lives that can distract us from His purposes. What is it that distracts you from doing God's will? It may be different from what distracts me, but God's Word has told us what to do during those times. God says, *"Don't look at it!* Lay it aside and press onward!"* If we'll just keep our eyes on Jesus, He will perfect our faith.

I had come to God in repentance so many times to ask Him to forgive my wrong attitudes and behavior that I finally cried, "O Lord, You must be tired of me coming to You in this way! I am so inconsistent in godliness! You never change! I want to be like You; You are constant in righteousness, altogether lovely and perfect in all Your ways."

(When we recognize the never-changing nature of God and compare it to our own nature, which is inconsistent in godliness, it will motivate us to get on our faces before God and ask Him to impart more of Himself to our character.)

Focus on His Consistency

As I cried out to God, He told me that He wasn't concerned about my inconsistency because He looked at the end product of what He was making me to be. He said, "I know that you'll always come back to Me, just like a puppy who always returns to flop at his master's feet, even after frolicking about foolishly." He said that He knew I loved Him and that His love would continue to grow in me. He said, "Within you is the potential to display My glory—just as I displayed My Father's glory—because I dwell in you."

God assured me that one day soon I would grow up, be loyal, and walk by His side at all times. He was simply asking me to trust Him, to completely yield to Him and rest in Him so that He could have my full attention. Only then could He clearly teach me His ways. He continued to tell me over and over again, "Get to know Me. I long to reveal Myself to you."

If we want to be like God, we must press in to know Him, for it is through intimacy with Him that He imparts His nature to us. As we are praising and worshiping God, there is a giving and receiving between our Father and ourselves. An interchange of love, joy, and blessing takes place. However, upon His lap is where we experience the impartation of His nature and find deeper communion with God. In that place of greater intimacy, He imparts His plans and joy to us. He places within us revelation of His will, and He imparts faith, hope, and joy to fulfill His will.

As we lean our head upon Daddy-God's chest and hear His heartbeat, He will always impart His very own heart to us. This is where we begin to understand the ways of our Father. The heart of God—His wisdom and compassion—must dwell within us if we are to be effective ministers of His love.

It is when we are in intimacy with the Father, when we are looking into His wonderful eyes, that God always imparts His vision to us. After Jesus healed the invalid at the pool of Bethesda, the Jews began to persecute Jesus and sought to kill Him because He was doing these things on the Sabbath (see Jn. 5:2-16). Jesus told them that He was not able to do anything of Himself, but only what He saw the Father doing (see Jn. 5:19). I believe the Father wants us to see what He is doing, and when He is doing it, so that we can do His works any time and any place, just like Jesus did.

Receive His Nature

Finally, it is in intimacy with the Father, as we put our arms around His neck and lay our head upon His shoulder (which represents His government), that we will find perfect rest in His Kingdom (see Is. 9:6-7). In that place of rest, there is always an impartation of His governing power and authority. God's impartation of His nature is very important for us individually, but it is also important for the purposes of His Kingdom. That is what our existence here on earth is all about! We are His daughters first and foremost because His love has chosen us, but His ongoing purpose is that we be a living demonstration of that love to the earth!

In Matthew 7, Jesus spoke of the importance of asking, seeking, and knocking on the door of the Father for the good and advantageous things from Him.

> *Keep on asking and it will be given you; keep on seeking and you will find; keep on knocking [reverently] and [the door] will be opened to you. For everyone who keeps on asking receives; and he who keeps on seeking finds; and to him who keeps on knocking, [the door] will be opened. ... If you then, evil as you are, know how to give good and advantageous gifts to your children, how much more will your Father Who is in heaven [perfect as He is] give good and advantageous things to those who keep on asking Him!* (Matthew 7:7-8,11 AMP)

When we seek Him, our heavenly Father generously gives to us all we need to demonstrate His nature and achieve His purposes in the earth. Jesus taught that the fruit produced from the lives of those who seek after Him would be recognized as excellent fruit and worthy of admiration. It is the fruit of our lives that reveals our identity and that of our Father (see Mt. 7:20). He also said that it is not simply those who call Him Lord who will enter the Kingdom of Heaven, but those who do the will of the Father who is in Heaven (see Mt. 7:21-23).

Until we come to the full realization and conviction that Jesus is Lord, until the King's rule is applied to our lives in everyday living, we will not be able to relate to Father God as we should. We need to seek Him and demonstrate His heart and Lordship to those around us.

When the time came for Jesus to be crucified, crowds that had once followed Him turned on Him. Even though Jesus was arrested, beaten, and killed, He made it perfectly clear that no one took His life. He chose to give it, and He did so that we might be reconciled to the Father (see Jn. 10:18; 19:11). The Father's purpose is that we might have close and intimate fellowship with Him.

> "The weaker we feel, the harder we lean on God.
> And the harder we lean, the stronger we grow."
> **Joni Eareckson Tada**

God doesn't throw us a life jacket when He saves us so that we can just float along the river of life. His intention is for us to become a part of that river! He desires that we function as a part of His life, giving Him complete ownership of our lives. Romans 12:1-2 tells us to conform our minds to Christ's ideas and attitudes in all things so that we can prove what is the good and acceptable and perfect will of God for each of us—individually and as His Body.

We can be holy like our Daddy-God, but there is a cost to holiness. The price is death: death to the ownership of our will and ways and death to our selfish desires and ambitions. We must choose to present our lives as living sacrifices, holy and acceptable unto God as we are instructed in

Romans 12:1-2. This is only reasonable! How could we present anything to God that isn't holy? It is so important that we make the choice to die daily so that Christ can live through us (see Gal. 2:20). God has brought us into His royal family, given us all things, and now His grace is teaching us to deny ungodliness so that we can walk in His ways (see Tit. 2:11-12).

The Church has not always functioned as God intended for it to function—as a pure holy Bride without spot or wrinkle. Many Christians do not have a zeal or passion for God or a desire to walk in holiness and in devotion to His purposes. Yet, God has such a wonderful plan for His Church, a plan that includes a beautiful purpose for each one of His daughters. We must understand whose we are and allow Him to transform us so that we may reflect His heart and nature. It is time that we, as believers, obediently bear His authority and power in the earth and fulfill His purpose for this generation.

We are daughters of the King of kings, the King who shall reign forever and ever (see Rev. 11:15). As His daughters, we are truly women of royalty.

Chapter 2

Relating to Daddy-God

Our Father in Heaven is the perfect Father "from Whom all fatherhood takes its title and derives its name" (Eph. 3:15b AMP). Because we are God's children, everything that belongs to Him is ours! Our Father is not selfish or stingy. He longs for us to know and experience the fullness of the inheritance that He has for us.

When Daddy-God adopted us, He received us just the way He found us. However, because we have now become *royalty*, we will still need to go through a great deal of grooming and perfecting. We have not merely become royal ambassadors of the eternal God, but because we're His children, we have become ambassadors of the highest form. As we bring messages of reconciliation and peace with God to others, we are to bring it through a dramatic demonstration of who He is!

Seek to Please the Father

As daughters of the King, we represent the King's nature and character. God is love, and His love covers a multitude of sins (see Prov. 10:12). The only way that we can truly care for and minister to people is through the love of God.

Even though we are in the world, we are no longer "of" the world (see Jn. 17:14-16). However, our character is not changed the moment we get saved. As we began to see in the last chapter, change comes as we become intimately acquainted with our Father and learn His ways.

One of my fondest memories of my childhood is of talking with my daddy while I sat upon his lap. This seemed to be our highest form of intimacy. Because his face would be so close to mine, as I looked up into it I would notice details about my father that I otherwise didn't notice: the sound of his breathing, his own personal smell, the lines in his face, and the strength of his muscles. These were the times that I felt the closest to my daddy. He would ask me how my day was and if I had obeyed my mother. Often, he would reach into his pocket and pull out a surprise that he'd brought home to me. Of course, each of us received a little gift, but the individual attention he gave to each one of us kept our relationships with him unique and personal.

I still remember the time that my daddy gave yo-yos to my sister Nancy and me! This was a toy we had never seen before, so my father had to explain to us how to play with it. The thing that I loved the most about this particular gift was the time that he took to play with me, his daughter, as he taught me how to use it. Because my daddy got so excited that day whenever the yo-yo responded properly to my control, I practiced with it continually until I became quite skilled with it.

I remember my mother helping me to write special notes for him before I could read or write on my own. She'd place her hand over my hand as I'd write "I love you" on pictures I had drawn to put into my father's lunch pail. After work, when he came home, he'd say that the lunch hour had been the best part of his day because of the surprise I had given to him. Then, he would tell me how proud of me he was and that he had shown my pictures and notes to everyone at work. The joy that I felt from his favor was better than any gift he could have given to me.

My mother was an excellent example of someone who was loving to her husband and children. She always looked for ways to make each person in the household feel special. I remember my mother teaching me at only four years of age how to make Daddy a special snack from cold, sliced hot dogs and crackers, with catsup on the side. I loved to serve my father; he was the light of my life! When Daddy walked through the door after work, I'd seat him on the couch, serve him this fancy hors d'oeuvre with milk, then I'd perform a special song and dance just for him. When I finished, I'd curtsey, and I'd always end up on his lap afterward.

I'll Take What Pleases You

Because I loved Daddy, I wanted to please him and be everything that he wanted me to be. When I was a little older, my father worked second shift. Most of the time we ate an early dinner together, but there were times that daddy would eat his meal alone before he went to work. There were times when I would sit on his lap while he ate. He'd take a few bites of his meal, then give me a bite. Daddy loved hot and spicy foods, and he would often have a couple of hot peppers on his plate. When he would ask me if I wanted to try a bite, I would always say yes, and I'd act as if I loved them. Daddy would carry on and on about how I could eat peppers! Then, while everyone's eyes were large with disbelief, I'd eat more! I loved to prove to Daddy that I could handle the hot stuff. I understand now that I was saying to him, "Don't be afraid to give me what others won't take. If you like it, then I'll decide to like it!" Today, I enjoy spicy food and hot peppers because I acquired a taste for them while seeking to please my father.

When I grew older, I began to call my daddy, "Dad." This expression reveals that I thought I needed my father and his attention about half as much as I had needed it before. Of course, in healthy family relationships, parents do prepare and teach their children to eventually become independent. Children need to learn how to make decisions on their own. However, rebellion often teams up with independence and we lose the intimacy with one another that we once knew. I can't recount how many times I packed my suitcase and "ran away" in an attempt to scare "dad" into giving me my way. I would become infuriated when he didn't show any concern about losing me. I guess he felt I'd be safe while I hid in my closet for the 20 minutes or so that it took before I became bored.

When we are relating to Daddy-God, we must always remain a little child in our hearts. Our society conditions us toward independence. However, when we bring this mentality into the Church, it becomes religion. "Religion" is not a part of our Father's character. I once heard a conference speaker say, "The spirit of religion is legalism, opinion, debate, judgment, and criticism; that's the character of Satan! But your Daddy is mercy and grace, and we are to exhibit mercy and grace coming forth in a pure heart." When there is total dependency upon Daddy-God, we are enabled to "do all things through Christ" (Phil. 4:13). We will always be in desperate need of His constant care and direction. For me, God will always be "Daddy" because I will always be completely dependent upon Him. Once we begin to learn the ways of our Father and attain knowledge of His Word, we must be wise and guard against spiritual independence, remembering that humility is the "proper attribute of true wisdom" (see Jas. 3:13 AMP).

Daddy-God wants us to be secure in His love and acceptance, but He also wants us to think about Him and look for ways that we can please Him. When I served my earthly father his "snack" and entertained him, I'm sure it wasn't the quality of either one that held him captive. However, because

I loved my father and had excitedly waited on him to return home and had put a lot of thought into making him feel welcome, I served him "the very best" I could. This is what delighted his heart! God wants us to anticipate His presence!

We have our Father's assurance that those who wait for Him will not be disappointed: "But those who wait for the Lord [who expect, look for, and hope in Him] shall change and renew their strength and power..." (Is. 40:31 AMP). As we entertain His presence with our offerings and worship, we should offer Him our "very best." It's an honor to serve Daddy-God, and His Word tells us to serve Him with joy and gladness. That's what delights His heart! In Deuteronomy 28, God was displeased with the children of Israel because they were not serving Him with joy and with gladness. God said, "Because of this, you will serve your enemies" (see Deut. 28:47-48).

Sometimes God's children become frustrated from feeling as if they're always "under" and never on "top" (see Deut. 28:13,44). It is vital that we keep our hearts looking to Him and anticipating His presence, for devotion to God will cause us to serve Him with gladness!

> "Acceptance says, True, this is my situation at the moment. I'll look unblinkingly at the reality of it. But I'll also open my hands to accept willingly whatever a loving Father sends."
> **Catherine Wood Marshall**

The desire to like what God likes will cause us to trust Him in situations that might be too "hot" for others to take. God will never put anything into our lives that will destroy us, but the "hotter" it becomes, the more we'll be "hardened unto difficulties" for the future (see Is. 41:10 AMP). By trusting God in every situation and seeking to please Him in each one, we might even acquire a "taste" for the things that others would avoid. God loves for us to prove to Him that we can be trusted to handle difficult situations with grace.

Maturity Without Rebellion

Although we shouldn't grow toward independence in our relationship with Daddy-God, we should grow in maturity. When I grew up, I stopped trying to manipulate my father into letting me have my way through threats of running off. Even though I may not have always understood my father's ways, I learned to respect his rules. To rebel against him did not win his favor or promote his trust in me. One thing I have always known is that he only wanted what was best for me. Even when I thought he was wrong, he sincerely believed he was right and was looking out for my genuine needs and interests.

When we get angry with God and attempt to "run" from Him, He always knows where we're hiding! He knew where Adam and Eve were hiding from Him, and He sees you and me right where we are right now. He sees everything—even the thoughts of our hearts and the things that we'd rather not see in ourselves. His rule and judgments are perfect, and He is righteous altogether (see Ps. 19:9). We will mature only as we honor and submit to His will. As we continue to trust and obey Him, we will come to know, trust, and understand Him in even greater ways. We will know His character, and it will become developed in our lives as well.

God's character is manifested in who He is. He is love, wisdom, knowledge, grace, peace, and righteousness. He is always constant, and as we grow in intimacy with Daddy-God, He will manifest Himself through our lives. Intimacy with Daddy-God will develop the fullness of Christ's own stature within us to the praise and glory of God the Father. This is a picture of the Church that Christ is coming back for! It will not glory in itself, but its glory will be in knowing Him. As Jeremiah 9:24 (AMP) says,

But let him who glories glory in this: that he under-
stands and knows Me [personally and practically, di-
rectly discerning and recognizing My character],
that I am the Lord, Who practices loving-kindness,
judgment, and righteousness in the earth, for in these
things I delight, says the Lord.

I fully understand that I need God to impart His character into my life, but it blows my mind to think that He would
choose to make such a deposit into one so unworthy.
However, "His divine power has bestowed upon us all
things that [are requisite and suited] to life and godliness,
through the [full, personal] knowledge of Him Who called
us by and to His own glory and excellence (virtue)" (2 Pet.
1:3 AMP).

God wants us to know what we possess experientially,
not just intellectually. He has already given to us the mind
of Christ and His very own Spirit (see Lk. 11:13; 1 Cor.
2:16). Jesus prayed to the Father, saying, "I have given to
them the glory and honor which You have given to Me..."
(Jn. 17:22 AMP). My finite mind cannot comprehend such
love and purpose, but I thankfully and gratefully receive and
embrace it all, for Jesus said, "...it is your Father's good
pleasure to give you the kingdom" (Lk. 12:32).

The *Kingdom of God* is where His righteousness (right
standing with God and man) rules and reigns. It's where the
peace and joy in the Holy Ghost live in our lives (see Rom.
14:17). True peace and real joy can only come from God.
This peace and this joy are more than what we experience
from our salvation, for He gives us His very peace and joy!
As we find God's favor through an upright heart, our Father
rejoices over us (see Zeph. 3:17)! I believe God laughs,
dances, and sings over us because of His delight and great
love for us, and when He does, His peace and joy become
powerful, free-flowing rivers that overflow into us.

Jesus said, "I do not call you servants but friends, and everything that the Father reveals to Me, I will reveal to you" (see Jn. 15:15). God likes us! He not only loves us, but He *genuinely* likes us! God enjoys our company and wants to spend time with us. That's why the Lord continually draws us to Himself and tells us to come into His presence. He's saying, "Hang out with Me! Talk with Me! Fellowship and commune with Me!" First Thessalonians 5:24 (AMP) says, "Faithful is He Who is calling you [to Himself]...." Daddy-God calls us, saying, "Come, sit with Me for awhile. Tell Me what's on your heart. Tell Me what you are struggling with. I already know, but I want you to talk to Me about it. I want to impart wisdom to you in the things of life. Get to know Me!"

Make Time to Spend With Him

Sometimes we get caught up in busyness, like Jesus' friend Martha. Luke 10 records a time when Jesus, His disciples, and a few other friends were gathered at Martha's house. Scripture describes Martha the following way: "But Martha [overly occupied and too busy] was distracted with much serving..." (Lk. 10:40 AMP). I'm sure Martha felt it was a privilege to serve the Lord in hospitality, so she probably went to great lengths to prepare a delicious meal with all the trimmings. Martha expected her sister Mary to roll up her sleeves and work with the same passion to serve the Master as she was doing. Yet, while Martha worked herself into a frenzy, Mary sat idly at Jesus' feet.

It was not long until Martha was having a pity party for herself and had become very angry with her sister. Nobody seemed to be noticing how hard she had been working or that she was missing the spiritual lessons that the others were privileged to be receiving. Finally, in frustration, Martha said, "Lord, is it nothing to You that my sister has left me to serve alone? Tell her then to help me [to lend a hand and do her part along with me]!" (Luke 10:40b AMP)

Jesus corrected Martha's thinking, along with her loud spirit! He responded to her, "...Martha, you are anxious and troubled about many things; there is need of only one or but a few things. Mary has chosen the good portion [that which is to her advantage], which shall not be taken away from her" (Luke 10:41-42 AMP).

I'm sure that Jesus appreciated Martha's zeal to serve His purposes, but when He is speaking words of Life, there is nothing that is more important at that time. God wants our hearts and our devotion more than He wants us to work for Him. I believe that serving can be just as effective when it is kept simple. I think we should always give our very best; it's an expression of love, and if time allows for elaborate hospitality, great! However, the more elaborate the setting, the more preparation is needed before the time of visitation. Too many details can cause us to miss what is really important to our Father.

Martha was in the presence of God, but her busyness kept her from intimate fellowship with Him. I can imagine her attempting to lean her ear toward the Lord's voice while she was stirring the vegetables or arranging the dishes. She probably picked up a few words of wisdom here and there as she scurried around the kitchen. Maybe she stood by the door while the bread baked and heard a good portion of what Jesus spoke about during that time. However, because of her busyness, Martha was not able to focus solely on Him. When Martha became distracted by the cares of life, bitterness, anger, and self-pity destroyed the joy she had previously felt in His presence.

I can't recall how many times I've worked in God's presence, thinking that it would please Him, when all He wanted was for me to receive His words of life. Because I wasn't

pursuing His heart's desire for me, I became frustrated. I
acted just like Martha by feeling unappreciated and sorry
for myself. When I finally realized that "...the Word that
God speaks is alive and full of power [making it active, op-
erative, energizing, and effective]" (Heb. 4:12a AMP), my
mentality began to change. Martha was not thinking cor-
rectly, but she was thinking like many of us do. God's Word
is life to us, and it changes us! It's sharp. It separates the
mind and emotions from the spirit while it exposes, ana-
lyzes and judges the very thoughts and purposes of the
heart (see Heb. 4:12b AMP). As God's Word does its work
in me, it also does it *through* me. It makes me sharp and effective in ministering to the people to whom Daddy-God
wants to minister.

We all have responsibilities pertaining to work and life.
With so many different responsibilities, our priorities may
get messed up. However, we will keep our relationship with
Daddy-God fresh and vibrant if we remember that He does
not belong on a priority list. If God is the center of everything pertaining to our lives, then we can't lose our focus or
our intimacy with Him. Our relationship with Daddy-God
will continue to grow and mature until we reach the full
stature of Christ.

King David had an excellent relationship with Daddy-
God. In fact, the Father said that David was a man after His
own heart (1 Sam. 13:14). David said in Psalm 101 that he
would behave himself wisely, walking with integrity and a
blameless heart. He determined not to allow his eyes to
look upon anything evil and to stay on the path upon which
God had placed him. David decided to keep his heart clean,
not make friends with evil people, and have nothing to do
with those who sow discord. He pledged not to tolerate
pride, arrogance, and lying, but he declared that he would
look with favor upon the faithful and those who walked
blamelessly before God.

"God can make you anything you want to be,
but you have to put everything in his hands."
Mahalia Jackson

Although David was not flawless, he was able to behave wisely because he cultivated his relationship with Daddy-God. David kept his heart pure with all diligence through the intimacy he had with the Father. God was able to impart His nature to David and bring him to the place of His purpose because he sought God's counsel and trusted His words. As a result, David was able to declare, "You, through Your commandments, make me wiser than my enemies, for [Your words] are ever before me" (Ps. 119:98 AMP). David had better understanding and deeper insight than all his teachers, because God's testimonies were his meditation and because he had set his ear to hear God's precepts and his heart to receive, love, and obey them (see Ps. 119:99-100).

Our Father—The Never-Failing Hero

When my oldest son, Jimmy, was very little, he watched a television program called *The Greatest American Hero*. Jimmy didn't understand what a "hero" was, and he asked his father to explain it to him. After receiving the explanation, he looked up at his father and said, "Daddy, you'll always be my hero!" For years, Jimmy told his father that he was his hero. Looking back, I can see that as long as our son "kept his heart" in proper respect and honor toward his father, instruction and wisdom was easily imparted to him.

Relating properly to Daddy-God will always enable us to "come boldly" into His presence (see Heb. 4:16). Without humility and adoration, boldness would simply be obnoxious and arrogant behavior, behavior that God resists (see 1 Pet. 5:5-7). Daddy-God waits for us to wait for Him:

And therefore the Lord [earnestly] waits [expecting, looking, and longing] to be gracious to you; and therefore He lifts Himself up, that He may have mercy on you and show loving-kindness to you. For the Lord is a God of justice. Blessed (happy, fortunate, to be envied) are all those who [earnestly] wait for Him [for His victory, His favor, His love, His peace, His joy, and His matchless, unbroken companionship]! (Isaiah 30:18 AMP)

Daddy-God delights in being our hero. Let us come to Him, draw near to Him, seek to please Him, and submit ourselves to His Word. We will find joy and a relationship with Him that will transform us into His own beautiful image.

Chapter 3

A Spirit of Excellence!

In our society, productivity produces acceptability. It seems that the more we have to offer and the more we achieve, the more acceptance and admiration we receive in return. As we seek the approval and acceptance of those around us, we often utilize an invisible measuring stick by which we compare ourselves to others. And, of course, we usually come up short. We long for success, acceptance, and recognition, but many of us tend to focus on our weakness and our inabilities, which we compare to strengths of others. This imbalanced comparison often leaves us frustrated, wounded, and battling feelings of insecurity and inferiority. In this state, we usually do one of two things: We either withdraw from the people around us or compete against them.

When we become new creatures in Christ Jesus, we begin to learn to live our new life in a new way. However, if we do not strip ourselves of worldly thought patterns and behavior and if we are unsure of who we are as daughters of the King of kings, we may find ourselves striving to earn His acceptance and approval as well. We may battle against jealousy and comparison between the knowledge of God and individual gifts that we have and those of our brothers and sisters in Christ. Rather than living the life of peace and joy that our heavenly Father intends for us, we may find ourselves striving in the Kingdom of God like we once strove in the world.

> "In order to be a disciple we must deny ourselves...
> It means not death but life, not a narrowly circum-
> scribed life but 'abundant' life. The gate is narrow but
> not the life. The gate opens into largeness of life."
> **Elisabeth Elliot**

Although excellence is a good thing and is, in fact, the result of discipline and hard work, excellence in spirit does not come through striving. Striving for this form of excellence through the works of our own hands will even prevent us from obtaining it. We cannot earn God's love, for He gives it to us freely as His daughters. Neither can we strive to be exalted by God nor to gain the wisdom that only He can give. We cannot strive against one another and still succeed in God's purposes and God's will. It's important for us to understand what excellence in spirit is from God's perspective and how we can attain it.

Humility Is the Key to Excellence

In Daniel 5:10-14 (AMP), Daniel is described as having "an excellent spirit, knowledge, and understanding to interpret dreams, clarify riddles, and solve knotty problems..." *because the Holy Spirit of God was in him.* As Christians, we have the Spirit of God dwelling within us. And we are assured that this Spirit of truth who comes from the Father will testify to us concerning Christ (see Jn. 15:26). As in all things, Jesus Christ is our example in excellence. And in His example, we see the key to excellence and genuine success.

Let this same attitude and purpose and [humble] mind be in you which was in Christ Jesus: [Let Him be your example in humility:] Who, although being essentially one with God...stripped Himself [of all privileges and rightful dignity], so as to assume the guise of a servant (slave), in that He became like men and was born a human being. And after He had appeared in human form, He abased and humbled Himself [still further] and carried His obedience to the extreme of death, even the death of the cross! Therefore...God has highly exalted Him and freely bestowed on Him the name that is above every name (Philippians 2:5-9 AMP).

Christ-like humility will always cause us to be exalted, but pride will hold us back. The fourth chapter of James explains how pride and self-centered thinking leads to strife in the Body of Christ. The sensual desires, such as jealousy, coveting what others have, anger, and discontentment, cause us to war with one another (see Jas. 4:1-2). When we ask God to meet our needs but we don't receive what we have requested, it's because we have asked with wrong motives (see Jas. 4:1). We are selfishly and jealously seeking gifts and blessings for our own benefit without giving any thought to the purposes of God for our lives and for the Kingdom. If our intention is to heap pleasures upon ourselves rather than to further our Father's purposes, James says we are like unfaithful wives. We flirt with the world and its desires and behave like the enemies of God.

Yet we can change these behaviors through the power of the Holy Spirit. Like Daniel and the Lord Jesus Christ, we too can demonstrate excellence of Spirit. James 4:6 (AMP) says, "But He gives us more and more grace (power of the Holy Spirit, to meet this evil tendency and all others fully). That is why He says, God sets Himself against the proud and haughty, but gives grace [continually] to the lowly (those who are humble enough to receive it)." Again, the key to excellence is humility.

Before we can receive God's grace, we must first recognize that His nature is love (see 1 Jn. 4:8), and it is His love that motivates His grace towards us. "While we were yet sinners, Christ died for us" (Rom. 5:8b). We need to understand humility. Humility is not self-sufficiency, but lowliness of mind (see Phil. 2:3a). It recognizes the need for God, for His love and for His grace. It is demonstrated toward God through a thankful and grateful heart and toward people through thoughtful kindness and courteous behavior. Humility is based upon a sincere conviction that we are in constant, desperate need of God and His work in our lives. It also causes us to lower ourselves in our own estimation and to prefer and consider others above ourselves (see Phil. 2:3b). James 4:10 (AMP) says, "Humble yourselves [feeling very insignificant] in the presence of the Lord, and He will exalt you [He will lift you up and make your lives significant]." We truly find our significance in Christ through humility.

Learning to Die to Ourselves

I lived most of my youth and the first few years of my marriage crippled by insecurities and feelings of inferiority. I outwardly tried to appear as if I had it all together, but I lived in fear that I would somehow mess up and give away the truth that I was completely incapable of everything! As a young wife and mother, there was only one thing I did well. Because my parents modeled a loving and godly relationship, and because my mother was a tremendous example of submission, I modeled those things as well. I had the ability to do so because I truly believed in them. In the 1970s, family teaching was also prevalent, so as I applied myself to learning and practicing my biblical role, I matured in my ability and sincerity in this role with my family.

However, I'll never forget the afternoon God spoke to me and shook me from my comfort zone. With my house sparkling clean, I sat mending clothes while my children napped. As I sat there, I was mentally preparing our plans for that evening. Immediately following supper that night, my husband, who was the youth pastor of our church, would be lifting weights in the garage with three teenage boys. Therefore, I decided to have supper ready for our family to eat as soon as Jim came home that evening. While he spent time with the youth, I would clean the kitchen, bathe the children, and get them ready for bed. Then, after the boys left, I would spend the rest of the evening alone with my husband. As I sat pondering these thoughts, the Lord spoke to me and said, "I've called you to more!"

Now, caring for my family and home was all-consuming of my time. It was also my greatest desire and fulfillment! I quickly answered the Lord by saying, "There isn't time or room for more!" I felt overwhelmed by all my fears and inadequacies touching anything beyond my four walls. I could not imagine ministering outside my home. I quickly told the Lord that I knew He would rather I serve Him with quality than quantity. I was applying myself to fulfilling His calling to me as a wife and mother. There wasn't room for anything else. He responded, "Nevertheless, I've called you to more."

Finally, in surrender, I asked "How?" I was surprised when He said, "Lose your life in your husband, and you'll find it!" At first, I thought I was having a conversation with the devil, but then I remembered all the family teaching I had been devouring, and I realized that God was truly speaking to me. What took place over the next three weeks was the fruit produced through the work of the Holy Spirit within me.

Rather than having meat loaf with our family that evening as I had originally been planning, I invited the teen boys to come over early for a cookout. I played Ping-Pong with one while the hamburgers cooked on the grill, visited with another while I set the table, and read the funnies with the third while we waited for Jim to come home.

While the guys lifted weights in the garage, my three-year-old daughter and I served them lemonade. Then, as the boys were leaving our driveway, my husband, daughter, ten-month-old son, and I all waved good-bye. As I began to lose my life in what God told me to lose it in, I began to lose it in the purposes of God. As I lost my life in my husband's burdens, ministries, and pleasures, I found that they became my burdens, ministries, and pleasures also. (I believe that if I had been a single woman at that time, God would have told me to lose my life in something specific that involved ministry outside my personal arena.)

What God began teaching me that day, was how to die to self so that He could live through me. As I chose to lose my life, I began to find it. Without effort, I began to be released in the personality that God gave me when He formed me in my mother's womb. My insecurities and inferiorities dropped off me like leeches that had a match put to them! In three weeks time, I was walking with my head up rather than down. I was looking for people to greet and encourage rather than hoping someone would greet and encourage me. My shyness and fear of man disappeared, and no one was more surprised than I was!

When I looked over my shoulder and remembered previous weeks and years, I was impressed by what God was able to do with someone like me. Although I am still aware of my inabilities and inadequacies, I am now much more aware of God's adequate ability! Because of His love and His amazing grace, I can do all things through Christ (see Phil. 4:13). I am so thankful that when we hear God's still small voice and simply choose to obey it, He will *transform* our lives. We will become and achieve things we never dreamed possible.

Experience the Favor and Presence of God

God says that He dwells in the high and lofty place, but He also dwells with the person of a humble spirit (see

Is. 57:15). I believe we need to work hard at practicing humility. If we recognize the value of humility, we will quickly embrace it. Too often we stop embracing and practicing humility because it hurts. However, it hurts because we're cutting the flesh away! If we look for opportunities to humble ourselves, we will find out how much more of our flesh needs to die. As we allow this death, God's glory can then be displayed through our lives (see Phil. 3:8-10).

"God is always calling on us to do the impossible.
It helps me to remember that anything Jesus did
during his life here on earth, is something
we should be able to do too."
Madeleine L'Engle

Since God resists the proud, it is impossible for them to get close to Him. Striving is a form of pride. When we strive in spirit, we are trying to accomplish spiritual goals through our own efforts. When we strive in spirit, we become competitive and pushy, and the harder we try, the more insecure we become. Even though we may know God's love, we are unable to experience His favor.

Daniel was close to God. He had an intimate relationship with Him, made himself vulnerable to God, and completely trusted his life to Him even during captivity. Many of God's children today would mock God's faithfulness and throw themselves a pity party if they lost all that they had. They would become angry, blame God for their troubles, and stop speaking or listening for His voice. Some would forsake serving God and try to find whatever joy they could in the land of their captivity through new friends and new ways, even when those things went contrary to God's ways. However, Daniel didn't lean on his own understanding. If he had, he would have become discouraged and disillusioned. He continued daily communication with God, sought His wisdom through Scripture and prayer, and regularly interceded for his people.

Daniel *knew* his God, and because of that intimacy, he was able to do exploits (see Dan. 11:32).

When I say that I know someone, I am saying that I have a relationship with that person. I know more than just who she is; I understand and know more personal things about that person than just anyone would know. The longer and more intimately I know a friend, the more sensitive I am to that person's feelings. If something is troubling a close friend, I might walk into a room, look at her, and immediately ask, "What's wrong?" Because I know this person, I am able to sense emotions that others may not notice. The better two people know one another, the greater dependability and trust is established between them.

Because Daniel knew more than just who God was, he was able to put his trust in Him. Daniel not only had faith in God, but he had faith in God's ability to deliver him. Although he had been thrown into a den of lions, the next day Daniel was brought back out of the den, and it is written, "...no hurt of any kind was found on him because he believed in (relied on, adhered to, and trusted in) his God" (Dan. 6:23 AMP).

As we humble ourselves and seek God, we find Him and He reveals His secret plans to us (see Dan. 2:20-22). It is in Him that we will find the understanding, security, and peace that we need. Jeremiah 29:12-14 tells us that when we call upon God and pray to Him, He hears and heeds our prayers. When we seek God with our whole heart and inquire and require Him as our vital necessity, we will find Him!

The apostle Paul said that he counted everything as loss compared to the priceless privilege of knowing Christ (see Phil. 3:7). His desire was to actually be found and known in Him. He didn't desire to be known by any of his personal achievements, which were based on his own righteousness, but only by the righteousness that comes through faith in Christ. He wrote in his Epistle to the Philippians:

[For my determined purpose is] that I may know Him
[that I may progressively become more deeply and
intimately acquainted with Him, perceiving and rec-
ognizing and understanding the wonders of His
Person more strongly and more clearly], and that I
may in that same way come to know the power out-
flowing from His resurrection [which it exerts over
believers], and that I may so share His sufferings as
to be continually transformed [in spirit into His like-
ness even] to His death... (Philippians 3:10 AMP).

Paul sought to know God, and it was worth any price to
him to know the Father, share in His purposes, and become
transformed by the Spirit into His likeness.

Do We Know Our Father?

When my husband and I returned to God, as I shared in
the Introduction, we grew quickly in the knowledge and
various gifts of God. We were so hungry to learn that we attended every meeting our church offered. We counted it an
honor and privilege to serve the Lord in any capacity, and
we gave ourselves almost daily to fellowship with the
saints. Within two years after our return to God, we began
to be sent out as assistant leaders. We soon learned that our
job was to serve the pastors, encourage them, and help lift
some of the burdens they carried.

We were appreciated, loved by the people, and secure in
our relationship with God. However, one day while I was praying, I was flooded with the realization that even though I knew
God was my Father, I didn't *know Him*. I knew that I would
live eternally with Him, but there was so much that I didn't understand about His ways and the ways of His Kingdom.
Suddenly, I had a mental picture of myself in Heaven with
Jesus. I was in the midst of a crowd that surrounded Him in
praise. The people were all very important to the Lord. Even
though the huge crowd kept me at a distance, I would step onto

my tiptoes so that I could see Him better, and every once in a while, Jesus would look at me, smile, and acknowledge me.

As I watched this scene, I was overcome with tremendous weeping. I cried out to God, saying over and over, "You are mine and I am Yours, yet I don't even know You! I *want* to know You! I *need* to know You! I don't want to be just part of a crowd; I want to touch You and feel Your touch!" Suddenly, I felt the fear of the Lord so strongly that I trembled. I had never experienced the fear of God like that before or since that time. I then cried out to Him that I knew His Word said, "The fear of the Lord is the beginning of wisdom..." (Prov. 9:10), but I didn't understand it. The Bible also declares that we can understand all mysteries (see Eph. 1:7-10). However, here I stood as God's own daughter, and I did not even understand the fear I felt. I had been crying out for wisdom and knowledge, but I had no understanding of either! I told God that since He was my Father, I would not settle for just the knowledge of who He is; I must know Him (see Is. 9:6). My security and joy depended upon it.

As suddenly as the fear of the Lord came upon me, it lifted! God instantly began to answer the cry of my heart by filling my heart with Psalm 19. I began singing:

The law of the Lord is perfect, converting the soul:

the testimony of the Lord is sure, making wise the simple.

The statutes of the Lord are right, rejoicing the heart:

the commandment of the Lord is pure, enlightening the eyes.

The fear of the Lord is clean, enduring for ever:

the judgments of the Lord are true and righteous altogether.

More to be desired are they than gold, yea, than much fine gold:

sweeter also than honey and the honeycomb.

Moreover by them is thy servant warned:

and in keeping of them there is great reward.

While singing this song, I became frustrated because I couldn't remember all the words of the Psalm. I got out my Amplified Bible to find Psalm 19, but when I opened it, my gaze fell upon Proverbs 2. In this chapter, God answered every question I had asked Him.

> *...If you will receive My words and treasure up My commands within you, making your ear attentive to skillful and godly Wisdom and inclining and directing your heart and mind to understanding [applying all your powers to the quest for it]; Yes, if you cry out for insight and raise your voice for understanding, if you seek [Wisdom] as for silver and search for skillful and godly Wisdom as for hidden treasures, then you will understand the reverent and worshipful fear of the Lord and find the knowledge of [our omniscient] God. For the Lord gives skillful and godly Wisdom; from His mouth comes knowledge and understanding* (Proverbs 2:1-6 AMP).

I was truly crying out to *know* God and to have understanding and deep insight into His secret ways. First Corinthians 1:24 (AMP) says, "...Christ [is] the power of God and the Wisdom of God." God was telling me that if I wanted to *know* Him with the intimacy I cried for, I would have to pursue and seek after Him as I would for hidden treasures. The ways of the Lord are perfect, and I would find everything I needed for my success and happiness by seeking after Him. However, if I didn't desire Him in His fullness and determine to seek, find, and receive knowledge of Him, I would not find what my heart craved.

Excellence in the Kingdom

For the first time, I understood what it meant to be poor in spirit. Jesus said, "Blessed are the poor in spirit: for theirs is the Kingdom of Heaven" (Mt. 5:3). The Amplified Bible renders this verse as, "Blessed (happy, to be envied, and spiritually prosperous—with life-joy and satisfaction in God's favor and salvation, regardless of their outward conditions) are the poor in spirit (the humble, who rate themselves insignificant), for theirs is the Kingdom of Heaven!" Acknowledging this poverty of spirit, taking it to the Father, and trusting completely in Him to reveal Himself in and through us is the basis for developing excellence of spirit in His Kingdom.

> *He hides away sound and godly Wisdom and stores it for the righteous (those who are upright and in right standing with Him); He is a shield to those who walk uprightly and in integrity, that He may guard the paths of justice; yes, He preserves the way of His saints* (Proverbs 2:7-8 AMP).

God's ways are so precious that He only reveals the secrets of His wisdom to those who recognize their need and will crave and seek after it. He gives it to those who want the knowledge of His love to fill them and whose only motive is intimacy with God.

Because of the Holy Spirit of God, we, like Daniel, can be known to have an excellent spirit. The Lord has shown us what is good and what the Lord requires of us. It is to do what is right, to love kindness and mercy, and to walk humbly with our God (see Mic. 6:8).

It is only when we have humbly sought to know and obey our heavenly Father that we will find ourselves transformed and exalted. It is then that we will find our families and friends rising up and affirming the words of Solomon, "Many daughters have done virtuously, but thou *excellest* them all. Favour is deceitful, and beauty is vain: but a woman that feareth the Lord, she shall be praised" (Prov. 31:29-30).

Chapter 4

"Tell My Daughters..."

*"Are you still searching for Me
as you would for hidden treasures?"*

These are the words that God spoke to me as I stood in my kitchen wondering what had gone wrong in my life. I wasn't happy anymore, but I didn't know why. As my heavenly Father asked me this question, I realized that I had ceased searching for Him and I had become satisfied. My whole attitude was screaming out, "This is good enough!" and it showed in every area of my life.

I had become wounded while serving the Lord. I had become hard. I was still serving the Lord; in fact, my life was full of service, but I was frustrated, deeply discouraged, and disappointed. I told the Lord that I felt like a sponge that had once been soft and full of living water but had been wrung out and become hard and dry. As I examined my heart, I couldn't put my finger on exactly how this had happened, so I asked the *Lord* to examine my heart and to show me what He saw. I wept as He revealed to me that I had embraced an ungrateful heart.

> "Pain is inevitable for all of us,
> but misery is optional."
> **Barbara Johnson**

Sometimes when we've been hurt, we try to protect ourselves from becoming disillusioned or disappointed again. We hold ourselves back from becoming excited about things in life. We just exist. We isolate our hearts, and we stifle them in the process. To experience gratefulness, we must first recognize how blessed we are. When we do, we will rejoice in this life and give the best of ourselves to God and to others in all that we do.

Recognize the Great Treasures of Your Life

At the time of this revelation from my heavenly Father, I was married to the most wonderful man in the world with whom I shared three beautiful children. We were all healthy. We had a lovely home, and we were leading a church full of precious people. Yet, I was taking it all for granted due to an ungrateful heart. To *take for granted* means to assume without question or full appreciation. I grieved as I realized that this also meant that my family and my loved ones were not receiving from me the best that I could give to them. After I repented, the phrase "this is good enough" sickened me.

God wanted me to treasure Him and the gifts He had given to me. By my attitude, I had been demonstrating that I esteemed these gifts and relationships lightly. When I repented of my ingratitude, I again recognized the great wealth God had given me and the great treasure that I have in Him as both Daddy and King. I realized that I wanted to draw even closer to Him and experience more of what He had for me. As long as I was satisfied with what I had, I wouldn't take the time or energy to pursue Him or to prepare for His presence or to delight in His love as His beloved daughter. When I repented of my ingratitude, He graciously restored my joy and brought new healing to my heart.

Prepare for the Presence of the King

Later that day, I began to prepare to beautify myself for a special evening with my husband. I decided to put the children to bed early that night, prepare a candlelight dinner, fix my hair and makeup "just so," and wear my prettiest outfit. My thoughts were on pleasing Jim when I heard the Lord speak to me. He said, "Tell My daughters to prepare themselves to come into the presence of their King and their Lord."

As God's children, I know that we come into His presence daily. Hebrews 4:16 also tells us to come boldly into His presence. But in that moment, God was speaking to me. He was telling me that we need to prepare ourselves before coming before Him into His presence. As I considered His words, I wondered, *What does God mean? How do we do this?*

The Lord reminded me of the Book of Esther. There we are told of the most beautiful women in that land going through beauty treatments for 12 months before they were presented to the king. Likewise, God explained to me that He wants us to begin spiritual beauty treatments so that we might worship Him in the beauty of holiness; the continual application of these treatments will produce lasting results. The Lord led me to read the Book of Esther and continued to reveal to me His intentions regarding this issue.

King Ahasuerus ruled the Persian Empire from 486–65 B.C. His rule covered 127 provinces—from India to Ethiopia. The first chapter of Esther tells us that in the third year of his reign he made a feast for all his princes and his courtiers. This included the chief officers of the Persian and Median army and the nobles and governors of the provinces.

He displayed for them the riches of his kingdom for 180 days. That's a six-month party!

During the last week of this party, King Ahasuerus made a feast for the people living in Shushan, the capital city. He invited everyone, both great and small, to a seven-day feast in the court of the garden of his palace. The people of the capital city experienced royal life as they sat on couches of gold and silver that were set on mosaic pavement of porphyry, white marble, mother-of-pearl, and precious colored stones. He not only served the people the king's royal wine, but he served it in golden goblets. No one was compelled to drink, for the king had directed all the officials of his palace to serve only as each guest desired. He was a great and gracious host. As I read this, I thought, *What a nice man!*

As a little girl while I was growing up, I didn't feel this way about this king. I had always heard the story of Esther told in a way that made me think that he was quite a jerk. I felt sorry for King Ahasuerus' wife, Vashti, and I thought that she was terribly mistreated. My understanding and memories from Sunday school went something like this:

> "The king had been eating and drinking with a bunch of men. Mockery and disrespectful talk was being passed back and forth between them while they bragged about their sexual exploits and other things. Then, after the men were all drunk, the king told his servants to go and fetch his wife. He was going to exploit her by showing the men what a babe she was. Surely there would have been lust, woof whistles, and crude comments.

> "Of course, the Queen refused to come because she didn't want to be disgraced and humiliated. What woman who was truly a lady wouldn't feel the same way? Well, her refusal to come infuriated the king, and in his anger he had her crown removed and sent

her far away so that she would never see the king or be in his presence again."

However, as I began to read the Book of Esther anew, the Lord spoke to me and said, "Look closely." Verse 9 of chapter 1 says that during this special week Queen Vashti also gave a banquet for the women in the royal house that belonged to King Ahasuerus.

I saw that the king not only showed his people kindness and demonstrated his appreciation to them, but he also made sure that his wife, the queen, was given the very best to entertain with. His royal house and all that it contained was at her disposal! Esther 1:10-11 (AMP) says, "On the seventh day, when the king's heart was merry with wine, he commanded [his attendants] to bring Queen Vashti before the king, with her royal crown, to show the people and the princes her beauty...."

The phrase "with her royal crown" leaped out at me, and the Lord told me, "Her crown not only represented her dignity, but it demanded their respect." For the first time when I looked at this portion of the book, I saw King Ahasuerus as a king who wanted to share the glory of his kingdom with his wife. He also wanted his wife to receive some of the recognition for the success of the kingdom. I saw a husband who was proud of his wife and wanted his hostess to stand by his side while they said, "Thank you for coming. The party's over!"

Queen Vashti's refusal hurt and humiliated the king before all the people of the capital city. He had every right to be angered by her attitude. Proverbs 20:28 (AMP) says, "Loving-kindness and mercy, truth and faithfulness, preserve the king, and his throne is upheld by [the people's] loyalty." Not only did Vashti display disloyalty, but she made a fool out of the king before the people who loved and respected him. No wonder the king's advisors were concerned about the ramifications of her actions; by that evening, every wife in the country would probably cop the same attitude with their husbands. They could very well say, "Why should I respect you? Even the queen does not honor and respect her husband!" The advisors warned, "So contempt and wrath in plenty will arise." Since the breakdown in families always results in the breakdown of a nation, there was reason for concern!

Vashti had been queen of the great Persian empire. She had the privilege of knowing the king's heart and sharing intimacy with him. The king had given her all that she needed or could ever want in order to be successful, yet she took it all for granted. She assumed everything without question or full appreciation. This resulted in an arrogant attitude that caused her to be cast far from the presence of the king.

After Vashti was sent away, beautiful virgins across the land were sought for King Ahasuerus so he could choose for himself one who was far *better* than Queen Vashti. Among the virgins brought into the king's harem was a young woman named Esther. Esther was a Jewess who, after becoming an orphan, was brought up by her cousin Mordecai. He was an attendant in the king's court, so he was able to walk every day before the court of the harem to learn how Esther was and what would become of her. Mordecai loved Esther as his own daughter, and he instructed her not to reveal her nationality during this time.

Esther had such a sweetness about her that she immediately won favor with Hegai, the king's attendant over the harem. Hegai quickly gave her the things she needed for her purification, food, and seven chosen maids to serve her. He also gave her the best apartment in the harem. Hegai was "pro-Esther," and he wanted to see her become the next queen!

Beauty Begins With the Spirit

After the women finished their year of beauty treatments, they were to be presented one by one to King Ahasuerus. The king would not see any of them until they had prepared themselves. The king would not settle for, "This is good enough." They were required to take seriously the privilege of being chosen and to be grateful for the honor to be in his presence.

When the time came for a woman to be presented to the king, she was able to choose anything she wanted from the harem to take with her. Each could prepare and beautify herself according to what she thought would make her stand out among all the rest of the women. This would have included clothing, jewelry, and any kind of adornment.

I once thought of this process as one big beauty pageant! I believe these women were all beautiful, but I no longer think that was the main focus. Vashti was beautiful, and when the king remembered her beauty, he truly missed her. However, what the king desired was a queen who was far better in attitude than Vashti. He longed for a loving wife with a grateful heart. He wanted a wife that his heart could trust, one who would do him good all the days of his life (see Prov. 31:12).

The other virgins chose elaborate adorning, but Esther 2:15 (AMP) says that Esther "...required nothing but what Hegai the king's attendant, the keeper of the women, suggested. And Esther won favor in the sight of all who saw her."

Esther wasn't anxious or worked up over her situation, nor was she wise in her own eyes. She possessed an attractive quietness within her spirit, and she had the wisdom to seek counsel from someone who knew what pleased the king. As a result of these things,

...Esther was taken to King Ahasuerus into his royal palace...and the king loved Esther more than all the women, and she obtained grace and favor in his sight more than all the maidens, so that he set the royal crown on her head and made her queen instead of Vashti (Esther 2:16-17 AMP).

Jesus said, "...For many are called, but few chosen" (Mt. 20:16 AMP). In the past, I had not clearly understood what Jesus meant by these words, but I knew that I wanted to be among those chosen. I want to wear the crown of His favor. I want His heart to trust in me, knowing that I will do Him only good. As I reflected on these words of Jesus, I asked the Lord, "If many are called, why are only a few are chosen?" Immediately He answered me, saying, "Because only a few are willing to pay the price." The price is complete abandonment to our own will and ways. It's letting go of the hurts and poor attitudes that try to creep into our lives. It's totally surrendering and adapting to all the requirements that the King has set before us without murmuring or complaining. It's embracing a grateful heart for the privilege of knowing the King!

"Real joy is sorrow accepted and transformed."
Hannah Hurnard

If we will continually seek after the Lord and not take His goodness for granted or desire His benefits for our own advancements, we will find grace and favor from God. We don't need to be anxious about God's purposes for our lives. We can trust the Holy Spirit to lead us and teach us His ways. If we ask Him to show us what pleases Him, His counsel will direct us into a deep and intimate relationship with the King.

God's blessing comes from being humble before Him, seeking Him as we would treasures, and fully trusting His purposes for our lives. A quiet, faithful spirit warms the

King's heart and pleases Him above other adornments. Let us each be grateful for the privilege of entering into His presence and take time to prepare to please and honor Him as the great, loving King and Father that He is. He is searching for a people who will worship Him in spirit and in truth (see Jn. 4:23-24). Let us search for Him and seek to please Him. Let us set aside our wrong thinking and wrong attitudes as we allow His Spirit to prepare our hearts for His presence.

Chapter 5

Preparing Ourselves
to Be Presented

"Lord, what must I apply to my life that I might walk holy before You?" I prayed. God had told me to apply spiritual beauty treatments to my life. He was calling me to worship Him in the beauty of holiness, but I needed greater directions on how to apply this to my life.

Give unto the Lord the glory due unto His name; worship the Lord in the beauty of holiness (Psalm 29:2).

I knew that the blood of Jesus had cleansed me and made me holy and worthy to come into His presence, but how could my life give the Lord the glory due His name? If I wanted my behavior to line up with holy conduct, I knew that I would *need* beauty treatments.

Beautified by Passion

"Love Me," the Lord answered. As I considered the words the Lord spoke to me, He reminded me of a prayer meeting that had been instrumental in teaching me about passion for God.

A church our family had been attending was praying for revival. Special time was set aside on Saturday evenings to gather together and pray. Only a few attended, and those few would spread out all over the building to find a private corner in which to pray. One Saturday evening I put my baby in her infant seat and sat her on the front pew where I knelt on my knees to pray. As I was praying quietly in my own way, a woman named Velda knelt at the altar nearby. Velda prayed aloud and with great passion about many things. Then she began to weep before the Lord. Lifting her face toward the heavens, Velda cried out, "I love You, Jeeesus!" Her face was scrunched up, and with great emotion she cried over and over again, "I love You, Jeeesus!"

Velda irritated me! I thought she should be ashamed of herself for making such a public display. Besides, she was making such a racket that I couldn't concentrate on what I wanted to pray about! Something began to stir in my emotions that made me very uncomfortable, and as I considered the situation, I recognized it as the old, familiar feeling of jealousy. Suddenly, I realized that I had an attitude problem. Velda really did love God; her whole life demonstrated it. Not only did she love God, but I knew that she had the love of God within her.

One plus in my life was that I was teachable and hungry for God. So, on the following Monday afternoon while my husband was at work and my baby was taking her nap, I knelt alone at my couch. I very carefully lifted my head toward Heaven, scrunched up my face, and cried out, "Jeeesus, I love You!" I repeated the phrase just like Velda did, "I love You, Jeeesus!"

Suddenly, the Lord spoke to me and said, "No, you don't."

Shocked, I told the Lord, "Yes, I do love You. There isn't a Christian anywhere who doesn't love God. Of course, I love You!"

Immediately, the Lord replied, "With all of your heart? With all of your soul? With all of your mind?" (See Matthew 22:37.)

Faced with a moment of truth and realizing that God knew everything, even the deepest secrets of my heart, I admitted that I really didn't love Him in that way. I confessed that I loved my husband more. I loved my baby more. And I loved some pleasures more. I confessed it all to Him as sin. I told God that I wanted to love Him as He had commanded me to, but I didn't know how. I didn't understand this love.

"Lord, teach me Your love," I prayed. For two years I repented for my lack of love and asked the Lord to develop His love within me. I've learned since then that the more I love God, the more He pours His love into me for others.

> "It's not how much we give
> but how much love we put into giving."
> **Mother Teresa**

I've always answered Justin's, my youngest son's, question of how much I loved him by saying, "With all of my heart!" One day when he was very small, he asked me if I loved him more than I loved God. I began to explain to Justin God's commandment to love Him above all things. I asked the Lord to help Justin understand, and then I told my son, "The more I love God, the more love He gives me for you and for others."

From that time on, Justin began cultivating his love for God. When I'd answer his periodic question of how much I loved him with the same answer as before, he'd always respond back, "Don't love me more than God, Mommy! Always love Him more than anyone or anything!"

God's top priority is that we love Him and that we know and understand His love. How can we represent God and demonstrate His attributes otherwise? Love is His nature.

First John 4:8 says that God is love. Of course, we need to beautify our lives with His love!

Love Draws Us Closer to Him

Shortly before Jesus was taken to be crucified, He prayed for His disciples and for all those who would ever come to believe in Him. One of the things He prayed for was that we would love Him in the same way that the Father loves the Son (see Jn. 17). Of course, all the prayers that Jesus prayed on our behalf are not only the Father's will, but also capable of being fulfilled. That's simply mind-boggling for me! I love the Lord, and I love to serve His purposes, but in order for His prayer to be fulfilled in me, I need a greater revelation of His love. I still need more of God's love developed and applied to my life.

When we love someone, we want to be with that person. Do you remember when you were pursued by someone who cared for you? I remember when Jim pursued me. I had met him while he was on a 30-day leave from the Marine Corps. We dated during that time and saw each other almost every day. During that time, we began to fall in love. His military base was stationed about two hours from my home, so when the time came for him to return to base, we felt as if he was moving far away.

As Jim was leaving, he told me that he would come home every Friday night to see me and then go back the following Sunday evening. You can imagine my surprise when he showed up at my door that Wednesday night. He said he just couldn't bear to wait an entire week to see me. Jim sacrificed time, money, and sleep so that we could be together for just a few hours. Within two months, he began driving home every night. He pursued me. He didn't pursue me to win my love; he already had my love. We desired to be with one another because of the affection that we felt. Love isn't always practical or even rational, but it will always cause other things to become secondary.

Blessed are they that keep His testimonies, and that seek Him with the whole heart (Psalm 119:2).

I remember when my friend Teri Beery once struggled in rising early for prayer. One morning while she was dragging herself down the stairs, the Lord said, "If 5:30 a.m. was the only time you could be alone with your husband, would you be excited about meeting with Bill?" Immediately, Teri responded saying, "Of course!" Realizing that this was her time to be alone in quietness with the Lover of her soul caused Teri to bounce joyfully down the stairs to her place of prayer and fellowship with God. Teri's mentality changed as she set her affection on things above (see Col. 3:2).

"Faith is a strong power, mastering any difficulty in
the strength of the Lord who made heaven and earth."
Corrie Ten Boom

Loving God and experiencing the reality of that relationship will cause us to be an enthusiastic people. Religion may allow Christ to be an aspect of our lives, but through intimacy with God, we will find Christ to be our life! Principalities and powers of darkness work hard to convince us that the world really doesn't want to know the Lord. Satan wants us to think that all unbelievers view Christians as "geeks." I was once convinced of this, but when I began to really fall in love with the Lord, I started to become enthusiastic about Him. I am now convinced that a people who love God will be an enthusiastic people—and enthusiasm is contagious!

Satan tries to convince us that it is strange or odd to be enthused about the Lover of our souls. If we buy into this lie, we won't ever be evangelistic. Ephesians 2:2-6 tells us that before we received our salvation we all walked habitually according to the patterns of this world that are under the control of satan. We conducted our lives by the passions of our flesh, and our behavior was governed by our corrupt nature. We were children of God's wrath and heirs of His indignation.

What a frightening thought and sobering revelation! However, Ephesians 2:5-6 goes on to say that because of God's rich mercy and intense love, even though we were dead in sin, God has made us alive together in fellowship and union with Him. God gave us the very life of Christ, raised us up, caused us to sit down together, and gave us joint seating with Him. Through Christ, we may come to the throne of Daddy-God and sit beside Him in the heavenly sphere as He executes His purposes in the earth.

Through His love God not only apprehended us from death and gave us eternal life, but He gave us all things— including a position in Him! Ephesians 2:7 (AMP) goes on to explain why:

> *He did this that He might clearly demonstrate to us through the ages to come the immeasurable (limitless, surpassing) riches of His free grace (His unmerited favor) in [His] kindness toward us in Christ Jesus.*

In light of this great truth, how can we help but be enthusiastic?

Passion Is Contagious

I am deeply in love with Jim, and sometimes people will comment on the affection they see between us. We don't try to draw attention to ourselves, but because our love is real and continues to grow, it is an obvious thing. Our love for each other often encourages others to love one another more deeply. Well, it should be the same way with the Lord! The love we have for God should be very evident, and it should be very natural.

Romans 1:16 says, "For I am not ashamed of the gospel of Christ: for it is the power of God unto salvation to everyone that believeth...." If we allow satan to intimidate us through those who are intimidated by our intimacy with God, we will lose our enthusiasm and boldness. If we lose that, our vision from God will become dim and dull, and we will have trouble hearing His voice.

A dear friend of mine, Karen Noe, is the director of the Pregnancy Care Center of Wayne County, Ohio, where I also have my office. When Karen and the staff took the stance of not being ashamed of the gospel, people began to get saved regularly at the center. We have never been obnoxious or tried to cram Jesus down anyone's throat; we just stopped being ashamed and embarrassed. Even the yellow page salesman who came into Karen's office to sell us an ad gave his life to Jesus before he left the building. Jesus is the answer to everything, and He is life! How can we help but enthusiastically love Him? And that love is beautifully contagious.

The Lord has been faithful to continue to teach me about His love. While praising the Lord one Sunday morning, our congregation sang Graham Kendrick's song, "We Declare That the Kingdom of God Is Here." The song continued, "The blind see, the deaf hear, the lame man is walking. Sickness shall flee at His voice! The dead live again and the poor hear the good news. Jesus is King, so rejoice!" My spirit was greatly moved as I sang this song, for I long to see the ministry of Jesus flow freely through His people while they demonstrate the Kingdom of God around the world. I want God to use me to reveal His great love, so I began praying, "O Lord, fill me with Your wisdom. Fill me with Your knowledge. Fill me with Your power, so that I might fulfill the purposes to which You've called me."

The Lord answered me, saying, "It is not My wisdom that will keep you. It is not My knowledge that will keep you. It is not My power that will keep you." Now that took me by surprise, for I know that God is all powerful! He continued, "...but My great love will forever keep you! Out of My love comes wisdom and knowledge and power. Love is the foundation and the root. If love fails, everything else will fall away. However, as you love Me and those around you, My love will be developed in you. Then, out of that passion and out of that intimacy, will come forth true wisdom, knowledge, and power!"

Keep Love First

The apostle Paul prayed that we might become deeply rooted and founded upon love:

> *May Christ through your faith [actually] dwell (settle down, abide, make His permanent home) in your hearts! May you be rooted deep in love and founded securely on love, that you may have the power and be strong to apprehend and grasp with all the saints [God's devoted people, the experience of that love] what is the breadth and length and height and depth [of it]; [that you may really come] to know [practically, through experience for yourselves] the love of Christ, which surpasses mere knowledge [without experience]; that you may be filled [through all your being] unto all the fullness of God...* (Ephesians 3:17-19 AMP).

Because the Lord has continued to teach me about the love of God and because He continues to fill and develop His love within me, I can say today, "I love Jesus more than I love my husband, more than I love my children, and more than any pleasure in this life. I love God, but I know that I don't love the Lord like I'm going to love Him!"

Jesus commended the Ephesian church for being hard workers. They were patient, yet they had no tolerance for wickedness. They tested and appraised those who called themselves apostles of Christ but were not, and they found them to be liars. They patiently endured for His name's sake and had not grown weary or fainted (see Rev. 2:2-4).

It sounds as if the Ephesian church was a wonderful group of people who served the purposes of God. I'm sure Jesus appreciated their zeal, but He did have one thing against them. They didn't love Him like they once had. Service and good works had taken the place of passionate intimacy with Him. The Lord told them to repent and start over again because *the most important thing to Him is a relationship of love*, not an intellectual love, but a diligent, pursuing, passionate love.

Because of ignorance, selfishness, or just plain laziness, I have sometimes forgotten my first love in Christ. I'm so thankful that God isn't looking for opportunities to beat on us for our failings, but He actively seeks opportunities to reveal more of His love to us so that we may become more intimately acquainted with Him.

Jim, my husband, provides for me. He watches out for me to protect me, and I know he would lay down his life for my sake. Jim has also patiently endured my silliness at times throughout our marriage! All the embarrassing moments he's had to live through over the past 31 years haven't caused him to faint yet. I truly appreciate Jim and all that he has done for me, but the thing that is most important to me and thrills me the most is his undying love. Because Jim loves me, he thinks about me. He calls me from his office during the day just to talk to me; he's very romantic and often plans special surprises for me. If all this were to stop, I know I would miss the love I had once known.

Love is a commandment, and love is action. Therefore love requires effort on our part. As we apply the beauty of God's love to our lives, we will watch it change us more and more into the image of Christ.

The Lord has said to me, "Continue to love Me. As you do, you will grow in My love, and My love will flow from you. As it flows, it will touch many people like a river flowing down a mountainside waters dry places. My love will become a refreshing flood. It will not destroy as flood waters do, but it will bring life and it will build. It will build lives and build relationships. It will heal and restore emotions and personalities. My love will change hearts and visions, and new hearts and new visions will be created from this flow of My love."

If we will love him with all our heart, soul, mind, and strength, His love will completely envelop us. It will consume us and become a living demonstration of God's love wherever we go. His love will empower us to fulfill the words of Isaiah 61:1-4. His love will set people free from bondage and fear. It will draw the poor like a magnet, it will calm afflicted minds and bring peace. If we will simply love Him with our whole being, His love will empower us to do His mighty works!

Beautified Through Yielding to Him

As we recognize the beauty of God's love, we will desire to yield to His will. The continual application of yielding to Him molds the beauty of holiness into our lives. As we look to God, we will learn of Him and from Him. We will be filled with whatever we desire. If we hunger after God, He will fill us with Himself. If our desires are self-seeking and self-serving, we will be filled with the frustration of walking in our own way. God will not pour what is clean into an unclean vessel. However, as we yield to God, we will experience His continual cleansing and filling of Himself and His love. We will only experience what we choose to walk in.

When I reflected on this concept, I prayed, "Lord, I thought I yielded my life to You the day I received my salvation. Yet I hear You say to me that another beauty treatment I need to apply to my life is yieldedness to You. What must I do to yield to You?"

I was expecting Him to reveal to me some deep, spiritual exercise, but He simply said, "Do not yield to temptation. Yield to Me, and you will know victory and power." How often have we failed to yield to God's voice in the things that seemed very small? Perhaps you have sensed God's gentle prodding to rise early in the morning to pray, yet your schedule will be full for the next 15 hours and you know you need your rest. So, you choose to ignore that prompting. The gentle prodding went away, but later, when you were reminded of it, you rebuked the spirit of condemnation. Trust and intimacy are built in the little things.

God's Spirit desires to abide in and through us at all times, but we grieve Him so often. If we genuinely desire to be filled with the presence of the Lord, we must yield to Him in prayer. Much will be accomplished through prayer. Peace and joy will come from spending time in His presence. He waits for us in the mornings. He waits for us throughout the day and in the evening. We run in and out before His throne, but what He wants is for us to lock ourselves in with Him. It is through these times of closeness and communication that our love will increase. Much will be accomplished as we yield before Him.

We are valuable instruments in God's hand. When we are totally surrendered and yielded to Him, He can use us to do everything He created us to do and to fulfill every purpose He has for us in His Kingdom. But when we are not yielded to Him, we are like a tool that needs repair or a blade that is dull—we cannot be as effective as He created us to be.

We will be used for the purposes of God in an accurate way when we are fully yielded to God. We will be able to identify and cut down false teachings and false thinking in people around us. We will speak words that prick the heart of the rebellious and minister healing to the wounded. When we are yielded to God, we will minister life and direction to all who come in contact with us. God will use our tongue, but it will not be the sharpest part of the tool of God. The sharpest, most effective part will be our love, for it will be God's love shining through us. If we do not abide in Him, He cannot use us (see Jn. 15:4-5). That's why God says, "Love Me! To the degree that you love Me, you will yield to Me!"

> "God isn't looking for golden vessels,
> He isn't looking for intelligent vessels,
> He's looking for yielded vessels!"
> **Kathryn Kuhlman**

God is looking for yielded vessels that love Him. He will be able to trust those whose passion is hot for Him because of their loyalty and devotion. God has many servants, but in this hour He is calling for those who will be more than servants. He is calling forth co-laborers! He is seeking for those who not only obey His commands and do His work, but have caught His vision and will walk by His side. It is these to whom God will impart His very glory. He will anoint them in a way never seen before!

As God's very own daughters, we have the ability and the privilege to represent our Father in all His ways. We can do the things He does, say the things He says, and accomplish every purpose God has destined us to fulfill (see Jn. 5:19-21). The more we love Him, the more we will yield to Him. The more we yield to Him, the more we will know Him. The more we know Him, the more we are empowered by Him. The more we are empowered by Him, the more successful we will be in fulfilling God's purposes.

Let us beautify ourselves with His love and yielded hearts so that we might give Him the glory due His name!

Chapter 6

Recognizable Beauty

It takes time for beauty treatments to produce a recognizable effect. Esther began a commitment to consistent discipline 12 months prior to her presentation to the king. The women chosen for this period of preparation did not vacillate in consistency; their routines were regularly kept. Since these were the most beautiful virgins in all the land, I'm sure many of them must have felt ready to be presented after just a few weeks of oil and perfume treatments. I mean, just how soft and sweet smelling can someone get?

However, more took place during that 12-month period than simply beautifying the outward appearance. During this period these women learned the ways of the king and his kingdom. The women learned patience, steadfastness, and faithfulness. Consequently, they experienced increase and results. At the end of that period, the final adorning was chosen for their presentation. Esther's final adorning was only what would please the king (see Esth. 2:15). So it should be with us as we prepare ourselves to worship the Lord in the beauty of holiness. We too must apply ourselves diligently and consistently to our preparations, to loving God more deeply and yielding to His divine will.

Preparation Is a Process

When I prepare to beautify myself in the natural by losing a few pounds of weight, I must give myself more than
just a few weeks. My whole mind-set has to change, and the
purpose is kept before me at all times. At the beginning of
this discipline, I'm the only one who notices the results. It
seems as if I can almost feel myself shrinking on the inside!
However, when I ask those closest to me, my husband or
children, if they can see a difference, their eyes quickly try
hard to see what they're supposed to see. I've learned that
it's best to simply and quietly endure my discipline and embrace patience until the change becomes evident. Actually,
I'm quite thankful for this because I know that if the change
was noticed too quickly, it would be too easy for me to become satisfied before I reached my goal. However, at the
end of my weight loss, others, including those whom I don't
know well, may comment on what they see.

The process of applying spiritual beauty treatments
works in much the same way. We will be the first ones to
recognize the changes taking place within our hearts and
minds. Although to us it appears to be already an obvious
thing, others may not see it yet. It's a good thing to testify
about the goodness of God and the things that He is dealing
with in our lives. However, if we talk too much about what
God is revealing to us and working in us before it is recognized by others, we may find ourselves spending time in the
pit like Joseph did (see Gen. 36–37).

Our beauty treatments must begin as a "God and me"
thing. It is vital that we close ourselves in with God as we
seek Him. As we discover more and more of His riches, as
our lives become saturated with His love and we continue to
gently yield to His purposes, our lives will begin to shine
from our newfound treasures. Before long they will be evident to all.

This spiritual process can be compared to putting on a nice ring. People may not notice a pretty ring, but if you keep on adorning yourself more and more with gold, silver, and precious jewels, you will soon become "Miss Sparkle!" The glow of these treasures cannot be hidden, nor will anyone be able to overlook them. Now, we wouldn't do that with natural jewels, and our spiritual adorning is not something we put on ourselves. Instead, God adorns us with the glory of His riches, and He lifts us up! Through Him we become as bright and shining as the new day.

Jesus told His disciples, "You are the light of the world. A city set on a hill cannot be hidden" (Mt. 5:14 AMP). When we take the time to prepare ourselves for our Lord, when we spend time and allow our Daddy-God, the King, to beautiful our hearts through intimacy with Him, strangers will recognize the beauty of the Lord upon our lives and they will desire to obtain this beauty for themselves. Jesus also said, "Let your light so shine before men that they may see your moral excellence and your praiseworthy, noble, and good deeds and recognize and honor and praise and glorify your Father Who is in heaven" (Mt. 5:16 AMP). As we mature and beautify our hearts, we will not only be Daddy's ambassadors, but we will cause strangers to the Kingdom of God to honor, praise, and glorify Him!

> "To keep a lamp burning
> we have to keep putting oil in it."
> **Mother Teresa**

After Jesus faced and overcame the enemy's temptations in the wilderness, He went to the lands of the Zebulun and the Naphtali people (see Mt. 4:1-17). These were people who didn't know God; they were complete strangers to Him. As a result of Jesus' faithfulness and obedience, the Scriptures say, "The people who sat (dwelt, enveloped) in darkness have seen a great Light, and for those who sat in the land and shadow of death, Light has dawned" (Mt. 4:16 AMP).

A Light and a Beacon

Because we have become "God's own purchased, special people," we are able to "set forth His wonderful deeds and display the virtues and perfections of Him who has called us out of darkness and into His marvelous Light" (see 1 Pet. 2:9 AMP). Paul says to God's children,

For once you were darkness, but now you are light in the Lord; walk as children of Light...For the fruit (the effect, the product) of the Light [consists] in every form of kindly goodness, uprightness of heart, and trueness of life. And try to learn [in your experience] what is pleasing to the Lord [let your lives be constant proofs of what is most acceptable to Him]. Take no part in and have no fellowship with the fruitless deeds and enterprises of darkness, but instead [let your lives be so in contrast as to] expose and reprove and convict them (Ephesians 5:8-11 AMP).

What a privilege to be called! What great potential and beauty is waiting for us as we prepare for our Lord and continually seek to abide in the presence of our King! We will be noticeably changed, and as a result, we will be empowered to bring change and hope to those around us. My prayer has been: "Let me be a bright light in this dark world. Let me shine with Your righteousness, drawing those in darkness to You so that You can lead them on."

Not every bulb has the same wattage. The degree of brilliance in a light is determined by the amount of power that is allowed to go in and then is released to go out. We also see various degrees of light in the Body of Christ. Acts 1:8 tells us that after the Holy Spirit came upon them the disciples received power ("ability, efficiency, and might") to be witnesses. The brightness of God in our lives is determined by how much of Him we have filled ourselves with. We can have as much of God as we want; we have His promise that if we will draw close to Him, He will draw close to us (see Jas. 4:8). As Fuchsia Pickett once said, "To the degree that we give up our own will, ways, thoughts, and ministry, can we have His!"

Expanded Not Extinguished

Life is not always fair, and it is often painful. Satan will try to capitalize on every situation that happens in our lives. Anything from everyday, run-of-the-mill things like small stresses or hormone changes to untimely things, such as a sudden death in the family, may become a target for his attacks. Satan desires to keep the power of God's love from flowing in and out of us. Since Jesus has already won the victory of our salvation and reconciliation to the Father for those of us who will accept it, satan will attempt to cause us to lose our sparkle. The devil hates us simply because God loves us. Since God has ordained for us to demonstrate His glorious praise in the earth, the devil wants to destroy this purpose in our lives. Satan knows that as the light of God's beauty is seen in us, others will be drawn to that light. That's why he continually wars against us.

From the beginning of time as we know it, satan has been in rebellion against God and at war against His purposes. He is the prince of darkness, the author of confusion, and the master of deception. His objective is to kill, steal, and destroy (see Jn. 10:10). But he cannot overcome the light of Christ and His purposes. The Light is more powerful than satan's darkness.

In the beginning [before all time] was the Word (Christ), and the Word was with God, and the Word was God Himself. ...: In Him was Life, and the Life

was the Light of men. And the Light shines on in the
darkness, for the darkness has never overpowered it
[put it out or absorbed it or appropriated it, and is
unreceptive to it] (John 1:1,4-5 AMP).

When our family received shocking and painful news of
the loss of our great-nephew to Sudden Infant Death syn-
drome, we entered a time of great mourning and loss. Not
only did we grieve for ourselves, but also for the parents and
grandparents who felt the pain even more deeply. Our associate pastor's daughter, Elizabeth, had married our nephew
Jason, and given us our first "great-nephew" Jacob. We have
been extremely close to each member of the family for
years, so the pain we felt for all at this loss was very great.
We cannot understand or know why this happened, but yet
we do know that this life often holds sorrow and heartache.
As the enemy came along and tried to use this loss to hinder and discourage our faith, God came to the situation and
graced it with His comfort and compassion, and instead He
strengthened our faith.

When we remember the story in Genesis of Jacob's son,
Joseph, we know he overcame many obstacles in life and became a great leader. The Lord once told me not to consider
Joseph to be an extraordinary man with an extraordinary
amount of grace from God to endure trials, but rather I should
consider him an ordinary man who was called by God to fulfill His purposes just as we are ordinary people, also called to
fulfill the purposes of God. Joseph experienced severe disappointment, sorrow, loneliness, and rejection from the time he
was a small child. He knew continual criticism, mockery, deception, and hatred from the ones he knew the most, loved the
most, and needed to trust the most. Joseph was forcibly separated from his beloved father, betrayed into oppression, and
subjected to ungodliness. He was falsely accused of moral
misconduct and sexual assault, and even though God's

grace was upon him for a prison ministry, he, himself, had a prison record.

How could anyone survive a life like Joseph's with such trial and suffering? Human reasoning tells us that experiences such as these would scar him for the rest of his life and that he would never be able to overcome the stigma of society. After all, his character had been destroyed in the public eye; how could he not be bitter? How could he ever trust again? Yet, Joseph was not spiritually or emotionally crippled, and he was eventually raised up in his own society as a leader and the final authority under Pharaoh. He was loved, admired, respected, and honored. Years later, when he saw his brothers who had betrayed him, he didn't hold bitterness in his heart against them, but said, "You meant it for evil, but God meant it for good" (see Gen. 50:20).

How can God use evil or hurtful situations for good? How can satan's attacks be made into victories for the Kingdom? Through our great-nephew's death, God revealed to us a greater measure of His heart for the lost. Oh, how we yearned to have little Jacob resurrected. We know that God is able to do all things and that Jesus is the same today as He was yesterday and will be forever (see Heb. 13:8). As we prayed and asked God to return Jacob to us, the Lord revealed to Grandpa Terry's heart the burden of the Lord for those who are dead in sin. The pain we felt and the longing we had to have this precious child returned to us is what the heart of God feels for thousands every day. We will see Jacob again, but each day thousands are lost and separated from God!

Because of our grief, satan thought that he might be able to dim our light for awhile and cause us to lose our sparkle. Instead, God took a sad and painful situation, gave us His peace, and caused us to shine brighter through intercession and evangelism. Through Jacob's death, God not only revealed to us more of His heart for the lost, but He also imparted a greater measure of His heart to us.

Since that time I have seen some of the greatest intercessors I've known literally weep and wail as if their hearts were breaking while they prayed for the dead in sin to know resurrection life through Jesus Christ. Jacob Sustar will be responsible for the salvation of thousands! April 1, 1998, marked the first anniversary of little Jacob's death. On that date we were able to commemorate his brief life with a memorial service in which we commissioned our new intercessors with the name "Jacob's Travail." From our loss is springing a source of life for others through the intercessions of God's people.

The trials of our lives can be compared to inoculation treatments, for such treatments are painful and might make us ill for a season, yet their purpose is for good. Any kind of disease is a horrible thing; there is nothing good about it. However, when used with wisdom, the same disease that brings death and destruction can be used for good to save many lives.

Trust the Father's Vantage Point

Small children cannot comprehend this because they aren't able to see the bigger picture. As adults, our thoughts and ways are too high and too complex for them. How can they understand how a painful injection of a needle that places a disease into their small bodies will make them healthy? Their bodies temporarily experience the disease, often reacting to the inoculation with soreness, aching muscles, and fever! It's not a pleasant experience for them, but caring parents know that it can produce good health and strength, and without it, they may become sick and die. That's why we allow this painful process to take place in their lives.

The same is true of our Daddy-God. We may not see the bigger picture, but we can trust that He does and that He is working each detail out for our good (see Rom. 8:28). He is perfecting and purifying our hearts and building our faith as we mature in Him.

Be assured and understand that the trial and proving of your faith bring out endurance and steadfastness and patience. But let endurance and steadfastness and patience have full play and do a thorough work, so that you may be [people] perfectly and fully developed [with no defects], lacking in nothing (James 1:3-4 AMP)

We can trust God not to give us a lethal dosage.

For no temptation (no trial regarded as enticing to sin, no matter how it comes or where it leads) has overtaken you and laid hold on you that is not common to man [that is, no temptation or trial has come to you that is beyond human resistance and that is not adjusted and adapted and belonging to human experience, and such as man can bear]. But God is faithful [to His Word and to His compassionate nature], and He [can be trusted] not to let you be tempted and tried and assayed beyond your ability and strength of resistance and power to endure, but with the temptation He will [always] also provide the way out—(the means of escape to a landing place)—that you may be capable and strong and powerful to bear up under it patiently (1 Corinthians 10:13 AMP).

There are many women who feel so beaten down by the enemy of their souls that shining brightly seems impossible, but it's not! No matter what has taken place in our lives, God knows the plans that He has for us: "For I know the thoughts and plans that I have for you, says the Lord, thoughts and plans for welfare and peace and not for evil, to give you hope in your final outcome" (Jer. 29:11 AMP). No matter what our circumstance, God wants us to allow His love to work in and through us, He wants to beautify us as we yield to Him. He doesn't want us to be downtrodden; He wants us to rise up! He has set His own light and love upon us, and with this, He has given us purpose.

In the early years of Queen Esther's reign, satan sought to destroy God's people through a man named Haman. King Ahasuerus had promoted and advanced Haman above all the other princes. King Ahasuerus had commanded all his servants who were at the king's gate to bow and show Haman reverence. Because Mordecai was a Jew, he would not bow to man, but only to God.

When Haman realized that Mordecai was not showing him reverence, he became so furious that punishing Mordecai would not satisfy his anger. Instead, he went to the king, and through flattery and manipulation, he plotted to destroy the entire Jewish nation. Haman deceived the king into believing that the Jews were dangerous to the Persian Empire because they were a strange people with laws of their own. Therefore, a certain day was appointed for the death of every Jewish man, woman, and child in all 127 provinces of the empire. Those who put them to death were to be rewarded by seizing the Jews' belongings as spoil.

When Esther's cousin Mordecai learned all that was done, he rent his clothes, put on sackcloth with ashes, and went out into the midst of the city crying with a loud and bitter cry. Then he stood before the king's gate, which was not permitted for anyone clothed in sackcloth. When Esther heard what Mordecai was doing, she immediately sent proper clothing to him through her servant. Mordecai explained to the servant what was going on and gave him a copy of the decree to destroy the Jews. He told the servant to ask Queen Esther to go to the king and plead for the lives of her people.

Esther sent a message back to Mordecai stating that this would endanger her life because the king had not requested her presence for 30 days. Anyone who entered the king's court without being called would be put to death. Only if the king held out his golden scepter to her would she live.

Then Mordecai told the servants to say this to Esther,

> *...Do not flatter yourself that you shall escape in the king's palace any more than all the other Jews. For if you keep silent at this time, relief and deliverance shall arise for the Jews from elsewhere, but you and your father's house will perish. And who knows but that you have come to the kingdom for such a time as this and for this very occasion?* (Esther 4:13-14 AMP)

As a result, Esther instructed Mordecai to gather all the Jews of Sushan, the capital city, to fast for her, having neither food nor water for three days and nights while she and her maidens did the same. She told him that after the three days, she would go to the king on their behalf—and if she died, she died.

When that third day arrived, Esther put on her royal robes and stood in the inner court of the king's palace. The king was sitting on his throne, and when he saw her, I think his heart began to flutter with love. Esther came boldly into the king's presence and immediately won his favor because of her beauty.

I once wondered what the big deal was really all about. After all, if the king loved Esther and she had been a good queen up to that point, why wouldn't he hand her the golden scepter? I could imagine her walking into the king's court, clearing her throat, and saying something like,

"Excuse me, sweetheart, I need to speak with you. Could you hand me that thing?"

However, the reason why it was such a big deal for the king to hold out his golden scepter was because that scepter represented the king's authority. Kings don't easily give their authority to others. In fact, men of any stature don't find it easy to hand over their authority to others—especially to women.

Quiet Grace Opens Doors

Many times Christian women are frustrated because they believe that God has called them to a ministry, but they're held back by the hand of man. Although this is often true, I think we can learn something regarding this from Esther's example.

After Queen Vashti was cast far from the presence of the king, a decree was sent out that all wives were to adapt themselves to their husbands. If a man were to marry a woman from another land, she was to even learn his language (see Esth. 1:20-22). First Peter 3 instructs wives to adapt themselves to their husbands in everything. It tells us, "Even if they do not obey the Word [of God], they may be won over not by discussion but by the [godly] lives of their wives" (1 Pet. 3:1b AMP). Peter also instructs women not to let their adorning be merely the beautifying of the outward appearance, but also the adorning of a meek and quiet spirit which is precious in the sight of God. I have also learned that this type of spirit is quite attractive to a man.

Esther had a meek and quiet spirit that brought her favor from all who had authority over her. She was not a weak or groveling woman; rather she radiated grace, gentleness, respect, and quiet dignity. Esther's spirit and attitude caused her to be raised to the position of queen, and it earned her the king's trust and favor. A woman with a meek and quiet spirit will be released to all God has called her to, and it will most likely be through the hand of man. In fact, male leaders who might have once held a woman back will be the very ones to open doors and honor her when she embraces a meek and quiet spirit. Their hearts will trust in her because of the beauty they see in her spirit, attitude, and behavior.

As the Lord began to deal with me more and more in regard to cultivating a meek and quiet spirit, I asked Him for an illustration, something I could compare it to. He had shown me the following verse from First Peter:

But let it be the inward adorning and beauty of the hidden person of the heart, with the incorruptible and unfading charm of a gentle and peaceful spirit, which [is not anxious or wrought up, but] is very precious in the sight of God (1 Peter 3:4 AMP).

I desired to better understand this verse. I knew that if a meek and quiet spirit was precious in God's sight, then women needed to embrace this principle. In response to my request for something I could "liken it unto," the Lord replied, "Clean underwear."

This not only sounded strange, but humorous to me. I laughed and told the Lord I just didn't understand. So He explained, "If someone chose to wear the same underwear for a couple of days, no one would know. However, if someone went day after day after day...you would not need discernment to know that something was wrong. Such a person would draw attention to herself and become quite offensive to others."

A meek and quiet spirit is the inward adorning and beauty of the hidden heart. It is not anxious or worked up, but it is gentle and at peace, fully confident that her Daddy-God has everything in His control. A meek and quiet spirit has nothing to do with the volume of the voice or the personality that God gave us at birth. It's a thing of the spirit. A woman can have a quiet voice and have a loud spirit and vice versa. Have you ever been in a room with someone who didn't say a word but who made you very uncomfortable? If it was not conviction you were experiencing, then that person's spirit was probably loud!

A loud spirit is anxious and overbearing. It is manipulative, usurping, controlling, and jealous! Whenever someone with a loud spirit is released into any kind of authority, you have a mess on your hands. However, a woman with a meek and quiet spirit will have the same effect on those holding authority as Queen Esther had on King Ahasuerus.

Esther's beauty had become so recognizable that it was the first thing that King Ahasuerus saw. He held his golden scepter out to Queen Esther at once. Esther had so great an inner beauty that it was reflected in her stance, her mannerism, and her speech. The beauty of her spirit was even reflected in her response to the king's extension of the scepter: "...So Esther drew near and touched the tip of the sceptre" (Esth. 5:2). I'd like to think that I too would have drawn near and gently touched the tip of the scepter. I'm afraid, though, that I might have quickly grabbed it with both hands and burst out, "Ohhh!...Thank you for handing me this thing. Now listen! I must have your undivided attention!" Yet even Esther's body language let the king know that she wasn't interested in his authority; however, she did have a request.

At this, King Ahasuerus said, "What will you have, Queen Esther? What is your request? It shall be given you, even to the half of the kingdom" (see Esth. 5:3). The quiet beauty of Esther's spirit won her such favor that the king was willing to share his very throne and kingdom with her.

Esther's beauty was also manifested in her wisdom. She realized that King Ahasuerus had been manipulated into believing Haman had the king's best interests in mind. She also knew that she needed the king's undivided attention before she presented her petition to him. At that moment his mind was probably preoccupied with the responsibilities and weight of the Persian Empire. So, even though she had already been granted any request up to half of the kingdom, her request was that he join her for lunch. Can't you just imagine her saying something like, "I've missed you, darling, can we spend some time together over dinner? And, sweetheart, please bring your friend Haman with you."

With that, I believe that she not only got his full attention, but his curiosity as well! As Esther left the king's court, he was probably thinking, "She's so cute, I can't stand it! She risked her life to have lunch with me. I've got to find out what's going on in her little head!"

King Ahasuerus told Haman to come quickly so that what Esther had requested could be done. Now she had them hopping! Her sweet femininity and gracious behavior probably had the king quickly sprucing himself before a mirror and splashing on cologne as he ran to meet with her.

As the wine was being served, the king said again to Esther, "What is your petition? It shall be granted you. And what is your request? Even to the half of the kingdom, it shall be performed" (Esth. 5:7 AMP). The king was saying to her, "Honey, my heart trusts in you! You know that I love you, so don't be afraid to ask me for anything. I want to give you whatever you want or need!"

Queen Esther's reply was, "My petition and my request is: If I have found favor in the sight of the king and if it pleases the king to grant my petition and to perform my request, let the king and Haman come tomorrow to the dinner that I shall prepare for them; and I will do tomorrow as the king has said" (Esth. 5:8 AMP).

Haman went away elated, thinking that he was honored above all other men because he had been asked to dine alone with the king and queen. However, remembering that Mordecai had the audacity to stand rather than to bow in his presence caused him to have a gallows made that were 75 feet high. He intended to go to the king the next morning and request that Mordecai be hung on them immediately. Then he could enjoy his special lunch with the king and queen that afternoon.

Yet that very night, because the king could not sleep, he asked that the book of memorable deeds be brought before him and read. In it was recorded a time when Mordecai had saved the life of the king by reporting two men who were plotting to kill him. Realizing that nothing had been done to reward Mordecai, the king decided to find a way to honor him.

So when Haman came into the court, before he could make his request, King Ahasuerus asked Haman what he thought should be done to honor someone in whom the king delighted. Of course, Haman thought the king was referring to himself, so he said to clothe him with the king's clothing, set him on the king's horse, and place a royal crown on his head. Then he said that such a person should be delivered to one of the king's most noble princes to be led through the open square of the city. This most noble prince would then proclaim before the people, "This is what is done to the man whom the king delights to honor" (see Esth. 6:7-9,11).

The king thought Haman's idea was great, so he ordered Haman to honor Mordecai in this way. Although Haman followed the king's command, he was so upset that afterward he ran home crying. Haman covered his head with mourning and told his friend and his wife what had happened. It was at this point that they all realized that because Mordecai was of the offspring of the Jews, Haman would certainly fall before him (see Esth. 6:13)! While they were talking, the king's attendants came to take Haman to the dinner that Queen Esther had prepared.

By this time, King Ahasuerus' curiosity was so strong that he was almost consumed with desire to know and fulfill what the queen really wanted.

And the king said again to Esther on the second day when wine was being served, What is your petition, Queen Esther? It shall be granted. And what is your request? Even to the half of the kingdom, it shall be performed (Esther 7:2 AMP).

Queen Esther answered him,

...If I have found favor in your sight, O king and if it pleases the king, let my life be given me at my petition and my people at my request. For we are sold, I and my people, to be destroyed, slain, and wiped out of existence! But if we had been sold for bondsmen and bondswomen, I would have held my tongue, for our affliction is not to be compared with the damage this will do to the king (Esther 7:3-4 AMP).

Even during this tense moment when Esther was revealing her nationality to King Ahasuerus and requesting her life and those of her people, she was proving to the king that his heart could trust in her to do him good. As King Ahasuerus' eyes were opened to the wicked schemes of Haman, he became enraged. What he thought had been the truth, suddenly came crashing down on him and was exposed as deception. So, while the king stepped outside for air to try to clear his mind, Haman began to beg Esther for mercy. He was so overcome by fear and panic as he pleaded for his life that he stumbled and fell upon the couch where Esther was.

This didn't look good! When the king returned from outside and found Haman on top of the queen, the king said,

"Will he even forcibly assault the queen in my presence, in my own palace?" (Esth. 7:8b) Later that day, Haman was hung from the very gallows that he had prepared for Mordecai.

A recognizable beauty like Esther's will make truth be heard and cause those who are in authority to protect what belongs to the King. As we allow God to work in our lives and adorn us with His beauty, we must realize that such change and beauty does not occur overnight. It comes gradually, just as the Lord's dealings and instructions come to us gradually. Yet, as we yield to Him, it does come.

Anticipate New Achievement

Real change is something that is built over time through prayer and time spent in the presence of God. My prayer continues to be, "Change me, change me, change me! Change my attitudes, change my living, change my level of faith, and change my level of righteousness. Take me higher into Your presence, higher into Your glory, and higher in anointing. Your Word says we have a high calling. Take me there, Lord! Burn up all the debris that gets into the way. Consume it all so that only Your works are displayed, only Your glory is seen, and the *beauty* of the Lord draws others to You."

As we allow God to beautify our hearts and minds through each situation and step of our lives, His purposes will be kept before us and we will move in them. This process brings a peace, and instead of walking in frustration, we'll move with anticipation! As we look forward to the great move of God that He is bringing upon the earth, we will perform His acts. We will be symbols of His beauty, light, and truth, and we will be prepared for all that He has for us. We will actually be carriers of His presence to a world that desperately needs His light.

Chapter 7

The Big Lie!

A Woman of Honor and Nobility

Kings' daughters are among Your honorable women (Psalm 45:9a AMP).

The psalmist declares that kings' daughters are honorable women. These women are given special recognition and are treated with respect. However, you and I aren't the daughters of just *any* king. Our Father is God! He was King from before the beginning of time, and He will be King throughout eternity! Since Daddy-God is King of kings and Lord of lords, certainly we are among the most honorable of women!

To gain a fuller understanding of this verse from the Psalms, I pulled my dictionary off its shelf and looked up the word *honorable*. It means, "in accordance with or characterized by principles of honor; upright. A title of respect."

Since the word *honor* is the root of the word *honorable*, I decided to look it up as well. *Honor* means, "honesty, fairness or integrity in line of beliefs and acts; a source of distinction, high respect as for worth, merit or rank." Another dictionary I own added the word *dignity* to this definition.

Now, I was on a roll! Excitedly, I looked up the word *dignity*. It read, "nobility or elevation of character; worthiness." This was getting more and more impressive, so finally, I looked up the word *noble* to better understand what this last definition meant. It read, "of an exalted moral character or excellence."

I couldn't help but rejoice as I copied down all these definitions. They not only define who we are as God's daughters, but they also declare our *success*. If we experientially know our honorable position, we will move in authority and power. We will go about destroying the works of the devil just as Jesus did (see Jn. 14:12-14; Heb. 2:14)! When we know and walk in our authority and power in Christ, we will know what it means to sit in the high places of the Almighty (see Eph. 1:19-21). Because of our intimacy with God, we will carry His glory wherever we go. Women who know who they are as daughters of the King and walk in that identity and authority will be given authority. They will convert sinners and teach them God's ways. These women will even have the ability to win unbelieving husbands to the Lord.

After writing down the last definition of *noble*, I realized that God has actually marked us with the imprint of His own likeness and royalty. I could actually feel God filling me with a new hope, expectancy, and mission. I began to believe with a higher realm of faith that I truly could do all things through Christ (see Phil. 4:13). However, when I glanced back at the dictionary, I noticed that the word following *noble* was *nobody*. The contrast from the previous words I had looked at made me laugh—until I read its definition; it read, "no one; a person of no importance, influence or power."

At that moment the Lord spoke to me and said, "This is who most of my daughters think that they are!" Suddenly, the contrast wasn't funny anymore. I could feel how this hurts the heart of God! When our Father adopted us, He purchased us out of darkness by His Son's own blood. He has made us light, made us holy, and has given us everything we need to walk worthy of our high calling. Yet, from my experience as a woman and from ministering to other women, I knew that this was true. Spiritually, most women feel like second-class citizens, and their low self-esteem keeps them from rising to their true stature in God.

Philippians 2:12-13 (AMP) urges us to enthusiastically serve God, "...[Not in your own strength] for it is God Who is all the while effectually at work in you [energizing and creating in us both the power and desire], both to will and to work for His good pleasure and satisfaction and delight." Most women's heart's desire is to obtain God's power to do His will, but they are held back and beaten down by what I call the "big lie."

The Source of the Lie

The "big lie" refers to the biggest and most effective lie satan uses to deceive God's daughters and hinder them in the Father's purposes for their lives. More women have embraced the lie that they are "no one; a person of no importance, influence or power" than have received the truth of who they really are.

The truth is, *we are women of value!* God is with us and in us, so we have nothing less than the Spirit of the Lord to impart to those around us. Christ in us looks to comfort, encourage, heal, deliver, and preach the good news of the gospel to the poor (see Is. 61:1-4). We are not unimportant individuals, but each of the King's daughters is a *somebody* with a great destiny to fulfill! Satan knows that we will arise and demonstrate in our lives what we believe about ourselves. In other words, if we believe we are a nobody, we will act like a nobody. If we experience and really *know* what it means to be a daughter of the King, we will act like royal, honorable women who have the power and love of Christ to share. Therefore, satan works hard to convince us that we have nothing to offer.

I asked the Lord what causes women to accept this deception. In response, a wave of emotions swept over me. I quickly wrote down each feeling. Then I began a survey. I asked several women if they regularly experience these emotions. One by one, I asked these royal daughters, "Do you feel *inadequate? inferior? lonely* (even in the midst of a crowd)? *foolish? embarrassed?* Do you feel a sense of *rejection* or *sadness?* And, finally, do you feel *disappointed?*

I was amazed at the outcome of this survey. Almost every woman I asked answered "yes" to most of these questions and some answered "yes" to all of them. Since that time, I have asked these same questions to women in different parts of the world, and the results have always been the same. Tragically, Christian women all over the earth are bound by feelings of inferiority, insecurity, worthlessness, and general unhappiness.

The Word tells us that God will generously give wisdom to us if we ask Him for it (see Jas. 1:5). I told the Lord that I was tired of being "had" by the enemy because I didn't see his attacks coming. So, I began asking my Father to reveal the strategies of the devil to me and cause me to be wise against his wiles and deceits (see 2 Cor. 2:11). Since I'm His daughter, I know God wants me to conquer every foe that would try to stop the mission that my Father, the King, has sent me out to fulfill. Ephesians 6:10 (AMP) tells me to be empowered and draw my strength from my union with Him. Since God is my Father, and the devil is my enemy, I need to see what God sees. Then I need to deal with the enemy as He would.

Be Armed With Wisdom

All of satan's plans against us are intended for the destruction of God's purposes. Why should satan have an advantage over God's daughters? If we remain in intimate fellowship with our Father, we will draw our strength through our union with Him. God has given us an armor to protect ourselves, but we must be sure to put it on like we've been instructed to do (see Eph. 6:11-18). For as we gird up our loins with His truth, we cannot be deceived! Putting on the breastplate of His righteousness protects our hearts from fear, deception, and sin. When we put on the helmet of His salvation, our minds are kept alert to God's purposes, and we will not fall short of them! As our feet are shod with the preparation of the gospel of peace, not only do we become ready to walk in peace, but each step we take strives to keep unity in the bond of peace (see Eph. 4:3)! Picking up the shield of faith in Him enables us to quench every fiery dart that the devil flings our way as he attempts to wound or immobilize us. Finally, the sword of His Spirit, which is His Word, empowers us with wisdom to completely destroy the enemy and his plans! When the Lord reveals the strategies of satan to us, God's wisdom and truth become the greatest weapons we could ever use in counterattacking the devil. Ecclesiastes 3:18 says, "Wisdom is better than weapons of war."

Many women seem to remain "stuck" with feelings of unhappiness and inadequacy because satan has unleashed spirits of dissension and deception against God's daughters to prevent them from knowing the Truth. Satan understands that when we *know* the Truth, we are set *free* (see Jn. 8:32). Jesus Christ proclaimed that He is the Truth (see Jn. 14:16). Daniel 11:32 (AMP) says, "...the people who know their God shall prove themselves strong and shall stand firm and do exploits [for God]." The New International Version says that they will "firmly resist" their enemy. If we lack intimacy with the

Truth, we will become subject to the lies of the enemy and fall prey to his ploy. But knowing the Truth enlightens us and gives us the strength that we need to display our *honorable* position.

I then asked God to explain how the spirits of dissension and deception keep women from recognizing their potential and position in Him. The Lord said, "The spirit of *dissension* works through a spirit of *irritation*, producing *faultfinding*. Then the spirit of *faultfinding* works through a spirit of *misunderstanding*."

When the spirit of *deception* is unleashed, it works to bring *wrong focus* to us. Then, *wrong focus* works through a spirit of *rejection*, and finally, the spirit of *rejection* produces *self-pity*. If satan can get us to this point, he will have us distracted. When we're filled with self-pity we feel hurt and usually reject and hurt others who come our way.

Lies Leave You Vulnerable

The whole purpose of this attack is to cause us to withdraw from one another. Because God commands a blessing whenever people dwell together in unity (Ps. 133:3 AMP), satan's strategy is to bring a curse by keeping us apart. The devil realizes that without love and unity, we will be ineffective. We will lack God's power, and without God's effectiveness and power, we are left feeling inadequate, inferior, embarrassed...and with nothing to offer—a *nobody*!

When I feel inadequate, inferior, lonely, foolish, embarrassed, rejected, sad, and disappointed, I don't feel like having fellowship with anyone. I don't feel like worshiping God, and I don't feel like praying. I don't want to gather with other believers. What I really feel like doing is having a pity-party!

When we're in this state, satan plays havoc with our minds and emotions. And when we find someone else who feels hurt, inferior, or inadequate like we are feeling, we have great potential for sowing discontentment, dissension, and discord. At these times, we're easily offended and often commit the sin of presumption with regard to our relationships. Presumption causes us to stumble over what we *think* others might be saying or thinking about us. We begin to believe these ideas as fact even though these offenses may never have occurred. In fact, most negative thoughts and feelings that hold us back in relationship with God and others are no more than *lies*! They really don't even exist!

Truth and Love Bring Unity

The Scriptures connect our love with our identity as children of the King:

> *Beloved, let us love one another, for love is (springs) from God: and he who loves [his fellowman] is begotten (born) of God and is coming [progressively] to know and understand God [to perceive and recognize and get a better and clearer knowledge of Him]. ... No man has at any time [yet] seen God. But if we love one another, God abides (lives and remains) in us and His love (that love which is essentially His) is brought to completion (to its full maturity, runs its full course, is perfected) in us!* (1 John 4:7,12 AMP)

Wow! The manifestation of God's love in our lives through relationships is satan's greatest nightmare and his worst fear. It is no wonder that the "big lie" is so high in his strategic planning. The enemy knows that our relationship with God cannot grow in intimacy or toward maturity unless we love one another.

Satan also understands how important friendships and fellowship are to God's daughters, yet the sin of presumption can prevent us from achieving them. Since loving one another is a key to intimacy with God and to the impartation of His nature, satan tries to keep us separated from one another. When the enemy stirs up waves of emotions, we withdraw from one another rather than turn to support and strengthen one another. This begins a vicious cycle that causes us to live in a way that is built upon the lies of the enemy rather than upon the truth of God.

Romans 12:9-21 instructs us to be sincere in our love with one another. Our love for one another needs to be the "real thing." As we embrace God's love rather than our wounds, His love will become power to us. The love of God will enlighten us, causing us to walk in His way, rather than in *a* way that merely seems right to our minds and emotions (see Prov. 14:12). When we follow His purposes, God's love will free us in our personalities and our love *will* be real and effective toward others. We will no longer stumble in our relationships or be the cause for others to stumble.

Ignorance to the truth of who we really are will cause us to listen to our enemy, the father of lies. When we believe his lies, our lives will become founded upon them, and we will become disillusioned. This should never be! Our loving Daddy-God's intention is to form us into His own likeness.

When people meet my only daughter, Jennifer, they often remark, "My goodness, I can sure tell that she's your daughter!" Not only does she look like me, but her mannerisms are a lot like mine because I have deposited much of myself into her. When our heavenly Father adopted us, He separated us from death unto life, and He immediately began putting His character into us. The visible manifestation of His character distinguishes us, His daughters, from the world. As we grow and mature as daughters of Daddy-God, we become recognizably His. This has been His plan and purpose from the beginning. It is part of His plan that He calls us to participate in.

For God so greatly loved and dearly prized the world that He [even] gave up His only begotten (unique) Son, so that whoever believes in (trusts in, clings to, relies on) Him shall not perish (come to destruction, be lost) but have eternal (everlasting) life (John 3:16 AMP).

By this we come to know (progressively to recognize, to perceive, to understand) the [essential] love: that He laid down His [own] life for us; and we ought to lay [our] lives down for [those who are our] brothers [in Him] (1 John 3:16 AMP).

Only as we forget ourselves and love others can Christ truly be formed in our lives. This is why the apostle Paul instructed us to regard one another better than ourselves and look out for the interest of others, for this is necessary for us to receive and demonstrate the mind of Christ and please the Father. (See Philippians 2:3-13.)

Grow Into His Grace

Before we can behave as the women of royalty that we are, we must first put aside childish, selfish behavior. Behavior that is self-seeking and self-serving will lead to self-consciousness, which results in the sin of presumption. Self-centeredness becomes self-consciousness when we overly concern ourselves with what others think about us. Let us strive for maturity and Christlike love!

[Let us]… all attain oneness in the faith and in the comprehension of the [full and accurate] knowledge of the Son of God, that [we might arrive] at really mature manhood (the completeness of personality which is nothing less than the standard height of Christ's own perfection), the measure of the stature of the fullness of the Christ and the completeness found in Him (Ephesians 4:13 AMP).

When I was a child, I talked like a child, I thought like a child, I reasoned like a child; now that I have become a man, I am done with childish ways and have put them aside (1 Corinthians 13:11 AMP).

Just as humility enables us to love God, it also enables us to mature and walk in love with one another. As we practice love, we will have no occasion for stumbling (see 1 Jn. 2:10). When we are offended by what we *think* that someone is saying or what we *think* they mean, humility and love will cause us to simply *ask* if our feelings are correct or if we have misunderstood. (I truly believe that if petty misunderstandings can keep the love of God from being formed in me, they just are not worth it.) I appreciate the opportunity to clear up an offense by explaining my heart to someone who has misunderstood what I've said or meant. This provides me with a chance to bring healing to someone I have wounded, which may have been due to a lack of wisdom or understanding on my part. Conversations of this nature teach me and correct areas of weakness and lack of understanding. By them, I grow in sensitivity and learn to choose my words more wisely. And if I have offended someone by being genuinely "out of order," I appreciate being called on it. Although it may not always be easy, I appreciate the opportunity to humble myself and apologize. In both cases, love is strengthened, unity is kept in the bond of peace, and the "big lie" is destroyed.

> "Kind words can be short and easy to speak
> but their echoes are truly endless."
> **Mother Teresa**

While praying about the broken state of many of God's daughters, the Lord showed me that many of His daughters have been like a cake that's been dropped along the pathway of life. Some have been stepped on, smashed down, and kicked aside as if they were nothing and worthless. Their

lives have not only been broken, but they have been seem-
ingly crumbled beyond repair. The "big lie" of the enemy
doesn't seem like a lie to them at all because every aspect
of their lives has been affected by the breaking, and many
of their relationships have been destroyed.

However, God does not abandon us, and He will not
leave us in our broken state. His love and power will remake
us, and the work will be a beautiful thing! If we allow God
to correct, mold, and reshape our lives, our very essence and
appearance will attract others to God. It will give them a
hunger for His presence and touch upon their lives. His
work will reveal His grace in our lives, and we will display
the glorious, creative nature of our Father.

Let Him Salvage and Transform

God told the prophet Jeremiah, "Arise, go down to the
potter's house, and there I will cause you to hear My words"
(see Jer. 18:1-5). Jeremiah did what God had instructed, and
when he got there, the Lord told him to look into the potter's window and tell him what he saw.

Jeremiah told the Lord that he saw the potter working at
the wheel. A spoiled vessel was in the potter's hand. It was
of no value or use, but the potter took that vessel and made
it over again as it seemed good to the potter to make it. The
word of the Lord that came next to Jeremiah can also be applied to every one of God's precious daughters:

> *O house of Israel, can I not do with you as this pot-
> ter does? says the Lord. Behold, as the clay is in the
> potter's hand, so are you in My hand, O house of
> Israel* (Jeremiah 18:6 AMP).

I once watched a video of a potter making a vessel. I
imagined myself as that piece of clay spinning around and
around. As I remembered and could relate to the times I
have felt like my life was going in circles. I thought, *No*

wonder I almost get dizzy when my focus is on the work and change that yet needs to be done in my life! Yet, the potter always stayed stationary, carefully watching and attending to his creation.

Interestingly, the potter continuously applied water to the clay throughout the entire forming process. Water is symbolic of the Word of God, and it is this Word that keeps my heart clean, soft, and pliable. Without the continual application of God's Word to my life, I could not be formed or healed from my brokeness.

Finally, the clay was brought up and shaped into what appeared to me a nice-looking and useful vessel. But, suddenly, the potter smashed it down to a mere lump again. I was astonished, and even though I was alone, I exclaimed, "What was wrong with that? It looked fine to me!"

There have been many times when I've thought that my "vessel" was just fine. However, the eye of the Potter sees every imperfection and flaw, even those that I'm unable to see. He knows the purpose for which He is making me, and not only do I need to fulfill this purpose, but I need to be made strong enough that I will not crack or break from the weight He has called me to carry.

When I saw the "smashing down" that the potter did to the clay, I also thought of some of the difficulties that God has taken me through. At times they seemed so hard and unreasonable, but now I see it is those very times that have strengthened me. God loves us so much; He will not settle for "this is good enough" in our lives. His work is always excellent and superior to anything we could imagine.

We need to remember that God sees us complete and finished through Christ Jesus. He speaks His intent over us and into us. He will take us from a lump of clay to a beautiful and useful vessel, from broken and undone to complete in

Him. However, we must first trust Him and be willing to get on His wheel.

After we have been spoiled by the sins and struggles of this world, God wants to make us over again as it seems good to the Potter. We must trust that our Father will not only "fix" our broken state, but He will make us better than new. John 8:36 (AMP) tells us that if the Son makes us free, then we are "really and unquestionably free"! Our Father is making us new, and He is making us free.

> *Therefore if any person is [ingrafted] in Christ (the Messiah) he is a new creation (a new creature altogether); the old [previous moral spiritual condition] has passed away. Behold, the fresh and new has come!* (2 Corinthians 5:17 AMP).

I can imagine the Lord saying, "You thought you were once a cake?" But rather than a nice little cake, I see each King's daughter as an elaborate and beautiful wedding cake displayed for the world to see its glory!

We must allow the full process of making and remaking to take place in our lives. When a cake is prepared, there are all kinds of ingredients necessary for a successful outcome. Of themselves, some of the ingredients are yummy. Others seem rather yucky. They may be either too bitter or too sweet, but the perfect mixture of these ingredients creates the *perfect* cake.

Perfected for His Purpose

His intention for our perfection is that we may be equipped to do the work of ministering, of building up Christ's Body, attaining oneness in faith (see Eph. 4:12-13). He wants us to truly know Him and fulfill all that He has created us to be—in our purpose and in our personality. After the making, we are *set free* for eternity to display the glory of the Lord.

God's work is glorious indeed! Psalm 45:11 (AMP) says, "So will the King desire your beauty; because He is your Lord, be submissive and reverence and honor Him." As we cooperate with His making, we will fulfill the Scriptures: "The King's daughter in the inner part [of the palace] is all glorious; her clothing is inwrought with gold" (Ps. 45:13 AMP).

God has clothed us with His own holiness and purity, making us "high in excellence and worth." As God's own daughters, let us reject and destroy the "big lie" by embracing and demonstrating God's love. Let us move forward in His purposes and become the dramatic, glorious evidence that our Father is King!

Chapter 8

"I've Chosen You— Come Forth!"

I was on a plane headed home after visiting my parents in southern California. As the wheels lifted from the ground, I heard an awful squeal. For the next 20 minutes, the plane shook, rattled, and squeaked. Then, for about 20 minutes before landing, the same thing occurred.

Before the plane landed safely, I sat in my seat wondering, *Will this plane go down? Will I return safely to my family? ...There's so much more I want to accomplish.* It was at that moment I realized how little I have accomplished!

I found myself asking God to forgive me for not appreciating life more. I began to ask Him for another opportunity to love my husband more dearly, mother my children more tenderly, and serve Him more devotedly. I thought of my mother who had just had her seventy-seventh birthday, and I imagined myself at her age and older. Suddenly I realized that no matter how old I get, I will probably ask the Lord for more time to accomplish the things that I've missed.

Just then, I realized that this is what God wants us to feel. It is not wrong to desire a long life on the earth. Our Father wants us to value the precious gift of life that He's given to each one of us, and He wants us to live life to its fullest. Unfortunately, we become caught up in worries, cares, and the value of earthly treasures far too easily, and we take the gift of life for granted.

> "God is the light of my darkness,
> the voice of my silence."
> **Helen Keller**

My husband and I both travel from time to time as part of our ministry. Although we often go together, sometimes one of us needs to stay home while the other travels. Separation brings the value of our lives and our relationship back into focus. It is in these times that we realize what a gift our 31-year marriage has been. We don't know how much longer we'll experience and hold our gift in one another, but we want to treasure every moment. This is very similar to God's intention for our very lives themselves, for when God breathed life into us, His intention was that we *live* for His glory while we wait for His return.

Few are chosen because few are willing to pay the price of self-abandonment! The times that I've laid down my will for His have been my moments of greatest joy and greatest reward. A time is coming when the Lord will wipe away every one of our tears. I believe that is when we will see how much we missed in life because our focus was on temporal things rather than on Jesus and His leading.

Beloved and Chosen Children

Jesus said, "You have not chosen Me, but I have chosen you..." (Jn. 15:16). In the past, I didn't really understand this verse because I felt that I had chosen the Lord. I specifically remembered kneeling with my mother at our living room couch at eight years of age and asking Jesus to come into my heart. As I looked at it, that was the day that *I chose* to become a Christian.

Now I see that before we came to Christ, we were like small, busy children, oblivious to God's love, until our Father picked us up from what we were doing. My third child, Nathan, was my strong-willed child. The Lord has given him an active and creative mind, and he was always into "something." I loved him so much that even though he may have been busy in his own little world, I would sweep him up into my arms and squeeze him for just a few moments. Sometimes I'd do this when he was about to run past me, and sometimes I would run after him. Of course, Nathan would acknowledge me the moment I grabbed him. At that moment, he would *choose* to give me a hug and kiss and say that he loved me, all the while struggling and kicking to get back to his busyness.

In much the same way, we didn't choose God until He chose us and captured our hearts. Even after that, we often struggle against Him because of our many distractions. When the Lord chooses us, He chooses us for a purpose.

> *...I have chosen you and I have appointed you [I have planted you], that you might go and bear fruit and keep on bearing, and that your fruit may be lasting [that it may remain, abide], so that whatever you ask the Father in My Name [as presenting all that I AM], He may give it to you (John 15:16 AMP).*

> *Even as [in His love] He chose us [actually picked us out for Himself as His own] in Christ before the foundation of the world, that we should be holy (consecrated and set apart for Him) and blameless in His sight, even above reproach, before Him in love. For He foreordained us (destined us, planned in love for us) to be adopted (revealed) as His own children*

*through Jesus Christ, in accordance with the purpose
of His will [because it pleased Him and was His kind
intent]* (Ephesians 1:4-5 AMP).

The first time I read the last sentence of Ephesians 1:5, I
laughed. People are always saying that they don't understand *why* God would choose us; and the answer the Bible
gives is, first and foremost, because He felt like it. It pleased
Him. Verse 6 (AMP) goes on to explain, "[So that we might
be] to the praise and the commendation of His glorious
grace (favor and mercy)...." Isaiah 60:21 and Isaiah 61:3
also tell us that we are the planting of the Lord in order that
He might be glorified.

God has called every one of His daughters to do great
and mighty things in His name, things that would be impossible without His power, things that will baffle and bog-
gle our minds. In these last days, Christ's Church will
display God's glory as never before. We need to be looking
to see what the Father is doing and then step out in obedience and faith to do whatever He tells us. We must decide
that we will obey, regardless of the cost. We must choose to
do what He has called and chosen us to do.

As we read the Bible, we see men and women of God
doing great things in His name. In this chapter, I want us to
consider just a few of these individuals. We must keep in
mind that these people faced the same types of feelings,
concerns, and inadequacies that we face when God calls our
name and chooses us for a specific purpose. God hasn't
called a few, He's called *many*. The choosing comes when
God sees that we love Him and trust Him enough to lay
down our own agenda to follow His.

Abraham and Sarah

Abraham told the Lord that he didn't have anyone to
carry on his name. God had been Abraham's friend; He'd

given him wealth, favor with kings, and many blessings. Yet even though Abraham had been very blessed, he had no child of his own to inherit his wealth and wisdom. When he took his problem to God, he explained that because he had no heir, everything he had would be passed on to his hired hand.

The Lord promised to give Abraham a son and sealed the promise by making a covenant with him. He assured him that his seed would be more numerous than the stars in the sky. When Sarah, Abraham's wife, first heard what God had told her husband, she was happy and looked forward to that day. She had seen the faithfulness of God in other situations and had already experienced many of His benefits. However, as time went on, her faith wavered because she began to focus on her inabilities rather than on the truth and power of the word of God pertaining to her life. Finally, she became convinced that she was incapable of fulfilling God's will.

Sarah still agreed with God's purpose and had faith in His promise, but because she was barren and beyond child-bearing age, she had begun to think as many of us would. She probably reasoned in her mind why she could not serve God in this way, thinking, *I can't do this. I really don't have the ability, strength, or faith to be used by God in this way, but I'm willing to help someone else fulfill this purpose.* It's a wonderful thing to support others in their ministry to God, but it's not a good thing to help someone else fulfill what *you* are called to do.

After failing in her own effort and laying aside her human reasoning, Sarah believed God again for His purpose in her life and trusted Him for the impossible. We need to remember that if God calls us, His intention is to choose us. God had called Sarah and chosen her to be the mother of a nation of His chosen people. He willed that she come forth in her calling. Even though Sarah had been barren all her life, was now 91 years of age, and her husband was 100 years of age, God showed Himself strong on her behalf:

> *Because of faith also Sarah herself received physical power to conceive a child, even when she was long past the age for it, because she considered [God] Who had given her the promise to be reliable and trustworthy and true to His word* (Hebrews 11:11 AMP).

What a tremendous testimony of God's grace concerning His will toward us. Our loving Father doesn't say, "Well, you blew it! You'll never see your inheritance now!" Instead, His grace teaches us, and His mercies are new every morning (see Lam. 3:22-23).

Moses

Moses was taking care of his father-in-law's sheep and took them around the backside of the mountain called the "mountain of God." He saw a fiery bush, and as he approached it, the Lord spoke to Moses, telling him to take off his shoes because he was standing on holy ground. God told Moses He'd heard the cries of His people, seen their oppression, and now He was going to deliver them through him!

Today, God hears the cries of people bound in sin and misery. Just like in Moses' day, God wants to deliver them and set them free, but He chooses to send His own children to speak and move on His behalf. When the Lord says that He is coming to demonstrate His power and set people free, we all rejoice. But if God would choose *you* to go free these people, you might feel as Moses did. His first response was, "Who am I?" (see Ex. 3:11) Abraham's seed had multiplied quite a bit, so much that their numbers had caused the Egyptians to fear them. Moses wanted to know, "Why me?"

God told Moses He'd be with him, but even more importantly, the Lord answered Moses' question by telling him who He was!

*And God said to Moses, I AM WHO I AM and WHAT
I AM, and I WILL BE WHAT I WILL BE; and He
said, you shall say this to the Israelites, I AM has sent
me to you!* (Exodus 3:14 AMP)

God made very clear to Moses all that would take place
with the children of Israel, yet Moses' focus was on his inabilities and fear.

*And Moses answered, But behold, they will not be-
lieve me or listen to and obey my voice; for they will
say, The Lord has not appeared to you* (Exodus 4:1
AMP).

Therefore the Lord then demonstrated to Moses that He
would be with him in power and through signs and wonders. God asked him what he was holding in his hand. It was
just his rod, but when he threw it on the ground as God told
him to do, it became a serpent. Moses quickly fled from it,
but the Lord told him to go back and pick it up by the tail.

I have to admit that would have been a difficult instruction for me to obey. I wouldn't want to touch it at all, let
alone pick it up at a place that it could still bend itself
around to bite or harm me in some way. However, Moses
did what the Lord told him to do, and the serpent changed
back into his rod. The Lord then told Moses to put his hand
into his bosom. When he took it out, it was leprous. God
told him to put it in again, and when he took it out this time,
it was restored and was like the rest of his flesh once again.

*[Then God said] If they will not believe you or heed
the voice or the testimony of the first sign, they may
believe the voice or the witness of the second sign.
But if they will also not believe these two signs or
heed your voice, you shall take some water of the
river [Nile] and pour it upon the dry land; and the*

*water which you take out of the river [Nile] shall be-
come blood on the dry land* (Exodus 4:8-9 AMP).

God chose Moses to deliver His people from bondage,
and even though Moses wanted them set free, he fought
God's choosing.

*And Moses said to the Lord, O Lord, I am not elo-
quent or a man of words, neither before nor since You
have spoken to Your servant; for I am slow of speech
and have a heavy and awkward tongue. And the Lord
said to him, Who has made man's mouth? Or who
makes the dumb, or the deaf, or the seeing, or the
blind? Is it not I, the Lord? Now therefore go, and I
will be with your mouth and will teach you what you
shall say. And he said, Oh, my Lord, I pray You, send
by the hand of [some other] whom You will send. Then
the anger of the Lord blazed against Moses; He said,
Is there not Aaron your brother, the Levite? I know he
can speak well. Also, he is coming out to meet you,
and when he sees you, he will be overjoyed. You must
speak to him and put the words in his mouth; and I
will be with your mouth and with his mouth and will
teach you what you shall do* (Exodus 4:10-15 AMP).

God will always meet us exactly where we are and will
help us through our difficulties. But just as it was with
Moses, if God has chosen us, we might as well agree in our
hearts to move forth in His calling. Once God has made His
choice, we really don't have one!

Deborah

When we look at Deborah in Judges, chapters 4 and 5,
we find a woman who was both a prophetess and judge. She
was contented to sit under her palm tree and minister to
those who came to her for counsel and judgment. After
prophesying to Barak to take 10,000 men to war with him

and saying that the Lord would give the enemy into his hands, Barak refused to go unless Deborah went with him. Now, this wasn't what Deborah chose to do, but she went because the Lord chose to send her and to show Himself strong through a woman.

As a result of her obedience to God, this woman, who had been ministering within a familiar setting and through the gifting and ability that she had become comfortable with, was suddenly stretched! Because of her obedience and confidence in God, she became a mighty warrior and victor for her nation. When God chooses us, He wants to use us above and beyond what we could ever imagine!

Jeremiah

In the Book of Jeremiah, chapter 1, the Lord revealed to Jeremiah that He had chosen him since before the foundation of the world. Before Jeremiah was even conceived in his mother's womb, God had chosen him to be a prophet to the nations. When Jeremiah realized what he had been chosen to do, he replied, "I can't speak!" and "I'm too young!"

God commanded him not to say he was too young, but to say whatever He commanded him to say. Then the Lord touched Jeremiah's mouth and put His words in him, saying,

See, I have this day appointed you to the oversight of the nations and of the kingdoms to root out and pull down, to destroy and to overthrow, to build and to plant (Jeremiah 1:10 AMP).

In verse 17, the Lord clarified Jeremiah's options with regard to his calling. He explained that if Jeremiah didn't do what He had chosen for him to do, he would be overcome by his enemies. Basically, Jeremiah didn't have much of a choice.

Like Jeremiah, many of us have a tendency to let our situations and surroundings affect our level of trust and confidence in God. When Jeremiah first began to minister in his
calling, he experienced what many would consider his
"high point" in his life as a prophet. For 19 years he was
well received as a friend and confidant of the king.

However, after King Josiah died, Jeremiah knew persecu-
tion and imprisonment with only brief moments of freedom.
He cried out to the Lord, "Everyone curses me" (Jer. 15:10
AMP). God would give Jeremiah His word for a person or
situation, and when he spoke it, he would be beaten and
thrown in jail. When Jeremiah held the word inside, it burned
like fire in his bones (see Jer. 20:9)! For a season of his life,
Jeremiah wasn't very happy with this difficult calling.

*Your words were found, and I ate them; and Your
words were to me a joy and the rejoicing of my heart,
for I am called by Your name, O Lord God of hosts.
... Why is my pain perpetual and my wound incur-
able, refusing to be healed? Will you indeed be to me
like a deceitful brook, like waters that fail and are un-
certain?* (Jeremiah 15:16-18 AMP)

Jeremiah had loved to minister to people, and he had
joyfully spoken and shared the word of the Lord. However,
because he experienced so much despair, his trust in God
started to waver as he began to question God's faithfulness
toward him.

As always, God remained faithful.

*Therefore thus says the Lord [to Jeremiah]: If you re-
turn [and give up this mistaken tone of distrust and
despair], then I will give you again a settled place of
quiet and safety, and you will be My minister; and if
you separate the precious from the vile [cleansing
your own heart from unworthy and unwarranted*

*suspicions concerning God's faithfulness], you shall
be My mouthpiece...* (Jeremiah 15:19 AMP).

God told Jeremiah that even though the people would
fight against him, they would not prevail over him, for the
Lord would be with him to save and deliver him! Our
greatest joy and fulfillment will come in embracing what
God has chosen for us to do. Remember, God chooses those
whom He loves!

Mary

Mary, the mother of Jesus, was visited by the angel
Gabriel who proclaimed the news that she, a virgin, would
conceive the Christ child. The angel's greeting to her was as
follows: "Hail, O favored one [endued with grace]! The
Lord is with you! Blessed (favored of God) are you before
all other women!" (Lk. 1:28 AMP)

Gabriel's greeting to Mary lifted her beyond where she
saw herself. She didn't lay in bed and think, "I am special,
aren't I? I've always known one day God would send an
angel to tell me how precious I was!" Instead, Mary felt
completely befuddled! Luke 22:29 (AMP) says, "But when
she saw him, she was greatly troubled and disturbed and
confused at what he said and kept revolving in her mind
what such a greeting might mean."

Mary didn't argue with God's choosing! Even though
she was aware of her own inabilities and inadequacies, she
responded, "Behold, I am the handmaiden of the Lord; let
it be done to me according to what you have said..." (Lk.
22:38). From that point on, Mary functioned in her calling
as the mother of Jesus. Truly, she is a wonderful example
to us all.

Peter

Peter loved Jesus! Of all the Lord's followers, he was probably one of the most demonstrative and outspoken regarding his love for Him. Peter was willing to lay down his life for Jesus. When the soldiers came to the garden to arrest Jesus, Peter was the one who quickly grabbed a soldier's sword and, before the soldier knew what was happening, cut off the ear of the high priest's bondservant. Peter was instantly ready to fight for Jesus. However, the Lord told His disciples to permit them to seize Him, and then He healed the man's ear.

What happened that caused Peter to curse his Lord while denying that he even knew Jesus? The Scripture tells us in Luke 22:54 (AMP), "Then they seized Him and led Him away, bringing Him into the house of the high priest. Peter was following at a distance."

When I read this verse, the last sentence leaped out at me. Because of his love for Jesus, Peter couldn't imagine ever turning his back on the Lord as Jesus had told him he would do. However, Peter was a "doer," and when there was nothing physically anyone would "do" to change the situation, Peter became frustrated and confused! He no longer walked beside Jesus, ministering to his Lord, but "followed at a distance." Whenever we follow the person of "Truth" at a distance, frustration and confusion are sure to set in. For when we do not keep truth close by, we will hear the deceptions of the enemy more loudly and clearly, and our own human reasoning will overshadow the truth.

Jesus had told Peter beforehand, "But I have prayed especially for you [Peter] that your [own] faith may not fail; and when you yourself have turned again, strengthen and establish your brethren" (Lk. 22:32 AMP).

I think the hardest thing for Peter to get over was probably his fear of failing again. He probably believed he could never trust himself again. He probably wondered how the Lord could ever depend on him again. Why should He?

Many of us can relate to the disappointment Peter felt in himself concerning his unfaithfulness to the Lord. Satan often uses our own weakness to hold us back from our destiny in Christ Jesus by convincing us to concentrate on our faults and failures. We need to remember that our faults and failures are why Christ died for us!

Peter received God's forgiveness, and just as Jesus had prayed, he then "strengthened and established his brethren." Even though he might have thought at one time that God would never want to use him again, God used Peter to preach the first message of "opening night" of the Church! This message is still being preached, as it has been for 2,000 years!

His Love Moves Us to Life

These individuals all displayed God's attributes and accomplished things they thought they were unable to do. Each had been called and chosen by their Father for a specific purpose, and in each case, it was *love* for the Father, not personal recognition and praise, that brought obedience.

We *must* get our eyes off ourselves! No one is able or capable of fulfilling God's purposes in his or her own strength or wisdom. Our declaration needs to be the same as the psalmist,

I will lift up my eyes to the hills...From whence shall my help come? My help comes from the Lord, Who made heaven and earth. He will not allow your foot to slip or to be moved; He Who keeps you will not slumber. Behold, He Who keeps Israel will neither slumber nor sleep. The Lord is your keeper; the Lord is your shade on your right hand [the side not carrying a shield]. The sun shall not smite you by day, nor the moon by night. The Lord will keep you from all evil; He will keep your life. The Lord will keep your going out and your coming in from this time forth and forevermore (Psalm 121:1-5 AMP).

God has made up His mind to fulfill His will through His redeemed people. Satan understands this, so he's gotten his entire force of fallen angels working overtime to keep us distracted by our human weaknesses.

There's an ailment called "Yea-but's disease" that needs to be annihilated from the life of every one of God's royal daughters. This mental illness keeps many persons disabled, depressed, and unable to rise to their potential in Christ Jesus. This disease flares up every time an opportunity comes to let God's glory shine from their lives. This disease presses individuals down until they become prostrate before their problems...as if in worship and obeisance to them. For these persons, their "situation" or "circumstance" always precedes the reason why they cannot come forth in their calling, immediately following the characteristic symptom of, "Yea, but...."

It's time for all of God's daughters to become healed and walk in the position and responsibility of their callings! It doesn't matter who we were, what we've done, or what has happened to us "before Christ." At this moment we are now His very own children and His own representatives!

Arise [from the depression and prostration in which circumstances have kept you—rise to a new life]! Shine (be radiant with the glory of the Lord), for your light has come, and the glory of the Lord has risen upon you! For behold, darkness shall cover the earth, and dense darkness [all] peoples, but the Lord shall arise upon you [O Jerusalem], and His glory shall be seen on you. And nations shall come to your light, and kings to the brightness of your rising (Isaiah 60:1-3 AMP).

God's glory was seen the day that Lazarus came forth from the tomb. John 11:5 (AMP) says, "Now Jesus loved Martha and her sister and Lazarus. [They were His dear friends, and He held them in loving esteem.]" When the report that Lazarus was sick reached Jesus, He stayed where He was two additional days before going to see him. By the time Jesus and His disciples arrived in Bethany, the town where His friends lived, Lazarus had already been dead and decomposing for four days.

Family and friends of Lazarus gathered by his tomb and mourned. Mary and Martha took Jesus to the tomb to join them. While there, Jesus said to Martha, "Did I not tell you and promise you that if you would believe and rely on Me, you would see the glory of God?" (Jn. 11:40 AMP) After a prayer, He shouted, "Lazarus, come out!" And Lazarus got up and walked out of the tomb, his hands and feet still wrapped in the burial cloths, and a cloth still covering his face. Jesus commanded the people to free him of the burial wrappings and let him go. (See John 11:43-44.)

Can you imagine the thoughts Lazarus might have had if he had been capable of thinking while lying there in the tomb. He may have had thoughts like, *How could God possibly use my life? I'm no good! I'm rotten to the core! In fact, I stink!* A lot of people feel this way about their life, that nothing of value could come out of it, because of what has happened to them in the past.

Jesus **called** Lazarus, and He **chose** him to **come forth** out of his past situation. He had more, an additional purpose, for his dear friend's life. He chose Lazarus to continue to be His friend and live his life to its fullest. He chose Lazarus to reveal God's glory and to demonstrate His power.

We are God's chosen and dearly loved daughters. When God calls us and chooses us for a purpose, we really don't have a choice. Disobedience always leads to death, so let's each respond to His call so that we too can come forth and experience *life* in its fullness!

Chapter 9

Get Ready... Get Set... Go!

Possess Your Inheritance!

The earth is the Lord's, and the fullness of it, the world, and they who dwell in it (Psalm 24:1 AMP).

Because the whole earth and all that is in it belongs to the Lord, every system in this world that defies the God of glory is operating unlawfully.

Today, God is calling His Church to actively and aggressively cross over into a place we have never been before—just like He called His people in Joshua's day. No longer are we to be settled, contented, and lethargic wilderness dwellers; it's time to dispossess enemies that the world thinks are greater and mightier than we (see Deut. 9:1-2). It's time for God's daughters and sons to take possession of the land that is rightfully ours.

It's Time to Move

How do we take back stolen ground? We do this by establishing God's rule in our lives and in the hearts of men! As we allow God's rule to be established in an area, satan loses power over that particular domain and the Kingdom of God receives its authority to fully rule and reign. Obedience to the King is the gateway to this land, and prayer establishes God's will. Listen to the words of God and follow them carefully; you will be amazed by the wonders you will see.

> *And now, Israel, what does the Lord your God require of you but [reverently] to fear the Lord your God, [that is] to walk in all His ways and to love Him, and to serve the Lord your God with all your [mind and] heart and with your entire being. ... So circumcise the foreskin of your [minds and] hearts; be no longer stubborn and hardened* (Deuteronomy 10:12,16 AMP).

I believe that God is calling us to recognize and embrace His mercy and grace in a fresh, new way. As we remember where we came from (the bondages of sin and our old destructive ways) and where God is bringing us to (His Kingdom, His ways, His love and truth), our hearts will be filled with praise and thanksgiving, helping to make ourselves ready for the battle of dispossessing the enemy (see Ps. 50:23). When our focus is on God's goodness and on His purposes, we will not take the work of the Holy Spirit or God's purpose for this work for granted. Instead, the reverential, worshipful fear of the Lord and a heart filled with praise and thanksgiving will motivate us. There is much for God's daughters to do in these last days! The days are growing short, and the time is at hand for the release of souls that are still enslaved.

"Is prayer your steering wheel or your spare tire?"
Corrie Ten Boom

While I was in a gathering that was praying for the harvest of lost souls, I received a prophetic word that seemed "out of the flow." I was afraid to give the word because it seemed to have nothing to do with what we were praying about. Instead, it was a strong word to the saints, saying, "My *people* perish for lack of knowledge!" (See Hosea 4:6.)

Even though I had read this Scripture before, the impact of what God spoke in that word shook my spirit. There we were praying for those who don't know God, and God spoke Hosea 4:6 to us! It says that God's own people are destroyed for lack of knowledge. When the priestly nation rejects knowledge, God also rejects them, and they can no longer be priests to Him (see Hos. 4:6b).

As I began to prophesy these words to the group, I saw someone standing on a path. The lighting around this person was as though it were dusk, just before darkness. I heard the Lord speak to that person and say, "You are in darkness," and the one on the path looked up and said, "I can see fine!" The reality of this thinking among many Christians also shook me.

Desire All of the Father's Will

Next, the Lord showed me a large buffet table and said, "You have approached My will and responded to it as if it were a buffet table. You have picked and chosen what you have desired to partake of and discarded what does not appeal to you. You compare yourselves with others, saying, 'I have partaken more of God's will than this one or that one.' You have felt full and contented, and therefore, establish yourselves in your own eyes, as sufficiently nourished. I call this rebellion and I call this darkness, for you deceive your own selves. *All* of My will is to be consumed!"

I believe that this is the hour of the lukewarm Church. We need to pray for the fear of the Lord to fall upon our hearts that we might be stirred and awakened to His purposes. This lukewarm current flows through many a contented, lethargic spirit. We know the Lord has already said what He would do with His lukewarm people; because He'd rather they be either hot or cold, God has said that He will spew them out of His mouth (see Rev. 3:16).

I believe the only way to get out and to stay out of being lukewarm is to repent of human thinking that justifies every reason why we "can't" obey some aspect of God's will. Then we must embrace the entire will of God, love it, and walk in it.

God has already shown up the nonsense and folly of this world's wisdom (see 1 Cor. 1:20). Human wisdom, or reasoning, leads to anxiety, which is a state of mental distress, concern, fear, apprehension, uneasiness, worry, and trouble. However, God's ways are much different; all paths of God's wisdom lead to peace (see Prov. 3:17).

> *But the wisdom from above is first of all pure (undefiled); then it is peace-loving, courteous (considerate, gentle). [It is willing to] yield to reason, full of compassion and good fruits; it is wholehearted and straightforward, impartial and unfeigned (free from doubts, wavering and insincerity)* (James 3:17 AMP).

The people of Joshua's day were told to choose life or to choose death. It isn't good enough to say, "Well, I don't want death, so I choose life." Deuteronomy 30:19-20 tells us that when we choose life, we are choosing to love the Lord our God, to obey His voice, and to cling to Him for He is our life and the length of our days.

Before Joshua led the people over the Jordan river to possess the land from their enemies, they were commanded, "Sanctify yourselves: for tomorrow the Lord will do wonders among you" (Josh. 3:5b).

The children of Israel were about to make some changes in their lives. No longer were they going to wander as they had before, but they were about to cross over the Jordan river, which represented death, and enter into a new life in God. They were commanded to set themselves apart because God was calling them for a holy purpose and was going to do a holy work in and among them. As the children of Israel crossed over Jordan, they left their old ways of life behind.

Today, God's people, His beloved daughters and sons, are about to enter into a new land. Our Father is speaking to us as He did to the people of Joshua's day, for we too must be willing to sanctify ourselves for a holy purpose. We are about to "cross over" from the life of sin and separation that we once knew to become a people whose hearts and minds are in unity with God and one another. Race, color, gender, and denomination will no longer divide the people of God, but as we love one another, our love will convince the world that Jesus is Lord!

I often ask women to consider their soul (the heart and mind) to be like a closet, and in this closet are many garments. In one person's closet may be a garment of rebellion or bitterness. Perhaps anger, resentment, or manipulation is hanging in that closet amidst a woman's other "clothing" that is being kept, just in case it is ever needed. The mind can always justify why there might be a "need" for those garments because human reasoning has everything to do with the emotions and human ways, and it is often in direct opposition to the truth and wisdom of God. This is why we frequently hear Christian people justify sin, saying, "If I went through what 'Sue' went through, I'd be bitter too!"

However, the wisdom of God has nothing to do with our emotions, but everything to do with the *will* of God. We need to choose to discard and get rid of every garment or attitude that might lead us into the lukewarm river. The clothing of anger, rebellion, and other attitudes of the soul described in the Bible as sin are not permitted in the pure river of God. However, they are not only acceptable, but popular items in the polluted river of the lukewarm.

"Choose You This Day..."

With each new day we have a choice of what garment we will wear. When we embrace the will of God even when it doesn't feel right, or seem to fit right, according to our human thinking, we choose righteousness. Often, it's at that moment that our "understanding" opens up to God's wisdom, because the path of the righteous grows brighter and brighter (see Prov. 4:18). The wisdom of God, the Word of God, continually operates as a lamp for our feet and a light to the path God would have us walk on.

God's ways are often very different from what we would choose or understand. Yet as we follow and obey Him, we experience greater depths of His love and presence in our lives. We are changed to become purer vessels of His Spirit and purpose. God is continually teaching me new lessons in this area. One rather dramatic example of a lesson God has taught me regarding obedience to His purpose and His overwhelming faithfulness occurred in connection to a ministry trip to Nigeria in 1994.

I had been invited to be a key speaker at a women's convention, and I had agreed to pray about it for a few months to ensure that God indeed wanted me to go at that particular time. I love to minister to the people of God, yet it is very difficult for me to be apart from my husband and children. However, when my husband and I prayed, along with our church leadership, we all felt that the Lord was directing me to accept the invitation and to go. Two months before the trip, several intercessors offered to gather and pray for the trip. I appreciated their offer but did not want to trouble them or tear them away from their families for special meetings. Just a few months before they had taken time to meet regularly to pray for another recent trip. Therefore, I declined their offer, asking simply that they remember to pray individually for me and the trip.

Peace in the Midst of Danger

I have often felt deeply homesick on ministry trips, and as the time for the trip approached, waves of emotion at times seemed almost overwhelming. Because the emotional struggle was so difficult, I began to question the word God had given about sending me on this trip. I struggled to hear from God regarding the words He wanted me to share with His daughters at this convention. My husband and I continued to pray and agreed that God would close the door if I was truly not to go.

A few weeks before my departure, I was deeply troubled by a night vision. For in this vision I saw my daughter Jennifer, Stephanie Biffert, and myself robbed at gunpoint by military guards.

I asked God if He was telling me to cancel the trip, but I received absolutely no answer. I felt only a deep dread inside, and I had absolutely no peace or joy with regard to the trip. The very thought of traveling to Nigeria upset me, and in tears, I told my husband that I could not shake off the feeling that I might not return home.

Jim immediately released me from going. He shared that he too had not felt peace about the trip for the past few weeks. I worried about my commitment and the difficulty that I would cause those who were putting the convention together. I thought of how I would need to seek their forgiveness for canceling such a commitment. However, as Jim and I talked and shared about this trip, we realized that God had not yet released me from going. We prayed again and asked Him to close the doors if I was not to go. Yet the doors seemed to be remaining open.

I began to hear many reports of violence in that country and surrounding areas. The unrest in my spirit began to keep me awake at night. I cried out to God to give me peace or to close the door for the trip. I listened for His voice, but I heard nothing—no confirmation, no new direction, nothing that would change the word He had originally given months earlier. Finally, I cried out to God and declared that although I did not understand what was going on, I would obey His original word to me. Unless He gave me new direction and closed the door to Nigeria, I would go...and if I died, I died.

Immediately God reminded me of the intercessors' offer months earlier. He asked me if I honestly believed that I could do anything without prayer. I confessed to Him that I could do nothing without prayer and repented of my foolish human reasoning. God had raised up these intercessors to cover me in prayer, and I had robbed them of being fulfilled in their calling and myself of their protective prayer covering. As I repented of my wrong reasoning and presumption, God filled me with His peace that surpasses all human understanding (see Phil. 4:7). This peace settled in my spirit and remained with me throughout the entire trip.

The vision of the robbery, the police, and the guns did take place during that trip, as did several other incidents that could have caused great fear, harm, and defeat. Yet, God's supernatural peace gave me courage and grace to rise to the demands of each situation. God faithfully preserved both myself and my daughter, and the enemy's scheme for evil became a testimony of God's grace and calling for that country, for my life, and for the life of my daughter.

Transformation Brings Revelation

We desperately need our minds to be transformed so that we can discern and follow His perfect will for our lives.

I appeal to you therefore, brethren, and beg of you in view of [all] the mercies of God, to make a decisive dedication of your bodies [presenting all your members and faculties] as a living sacrifice, holy (devoted, consecrated) and well pleasing to God, which is your reasonable (rational, intelligent) service and spiritual worship. Do not be conformed to this world (this age), [fashioned after and adapted to its external, superficial customs], but be transformed (changed) by the [entire] renewal of your mind [by its new ideals and its new attitude], so that you may prove [for yourselves] what is the good and acceptable and perfect will of God, even the thing which is good and acceptable and perfect [in His sight for you] (Romans 12:1-2 AMP).

We need to shed our old ideals and old attitudes. We are not to adapt or fashion ourselves to this age. Instead, we are to abound and be filled with the fruits of righteousness to the honor and praise of God, so that we might reveal the magnificent splendor of our heavenly Father (see Phil. 1:11). We have a responsibility to keep our hearts with all diligence (see Prov. 4:23), and to pursue God's ways above man's ways in all things.

God once spoke to me regarding human reasoning, saying, "Any time you mix the Spirit of God with human reasoning, you will produce a lukewarm people!" Although mixing our own wisdom with God's is common among many Christians, we need to guard against doing this any longer. To keep a pure heart, we must allow only God's Word to fill it. A pure heart understands God's ways because understanding is revealed while walking in them. A pure heart will love God and love righteousness. Those who have a pure heart also have the wonderful assurance that they shall see God (see Mt. 5:8). They will live for righteousness, stand for it, and be willing to die for it because Jesus Christ is our righteousness, and in Him is eternal Life.

"It was not weakness which enabled Him to become
a slave. It was not resignation that took Him

to Calvary. He had both accepted and willed
the Father's will."
Elisabeth Elliot

When a woman is about to be joined to her beloved in
marriage, she makes herself "ready" through various preparations. An important concern before that day is her
wardrobe. Before I married Jim, I went through my closet
and "trashed" every rag that didn't make me becoming and
beautiful in his sight.

After the people of Joshua's generation crossed over the
Jordan (from death to life), God commanded them to make
sharp knives and circumcise those of the children of Israel
who had not been circumcised during their 40 years in the
wilderness. Then God said, "...This day have I rolled away
the reproach of Egypt from off you" (Josh. 5:9a).

We, as a Church, are about to meet our Beloved in the
air to live and reign with Him forever. Even though God has
already sanctified us through the blood of Jesus, we must
choose to sanctify ourselves, and circumcise the foreskin of
our hearts and minds unto God. To get ready to enter into
the land and the types of relationships and service that God
is calling us to as His chosen daughters, we need to lose the
"sloppy look" and clothe ourselves with behavior belonging
to Christ (see Col. 3:10-12.). Christ is coming back for a
Bride without spot or wrinkle. In this final hour, we must
arise and sanctify ourselves. We must prepare for the release
of the harvest and help to prepare the Bride of Christ for
eternity with Him.

"Faith is for that which lies on the other side of reason. Faith is what makes life bearable, with all its
tragedies and ambiguities and sudden, startling joys."
Madeleine L'Engle

Revelation comes after we have cut away fleshly thinking. Revelation brings strength and establishes us. It also reveals what was hidden and where we're going. The truth of God's Word has been illuminated, and now that truth must be established and tested so that it can come forth from our lives as pure gold (see Job 23:10). When we are firmly "set" in God's truth, we will not waver, but we will remain strong in faith regardless of our circumstances.

Serving the purposes of God is the most exciting and fulfilling experience that we can have in this life. There is great joy in serving the King, yet there are also great battles to fight and overcome. For years, when circumstances surrounding me began to look bad, I would find myself doubting in my heart, even though I knew that all God's promises are "yea and amen" (see 2 Cor. 1:20). It's very easy to believe the truth of God's Word until we're tested in it. However, as the testing makes us strong, the conviction of our faith will travel from our head to our heart, and we will become set in His ways.

Enter Into Rest

Becoming set in God's ways also comes through rest. This is when we learn sensitivity to God's voice and His timing. For years, I would find myself becoming weary while serving the Lord. A state of weariness can often signify a spiritually dry place. Of course, this troubled me because Galatians 6:9 tells us, "And let us not be weary in well doing: for in due season we shall reap, if we faint not." Although I had not fainted, I was sure becoming weary.

I have observed three reasons for weariness in well doing, as well as three recognizable symptoms of it. *Discouragement, busyness,* and *a lack of recovery from being wounded* can cause weariness in well doing. *Frustration, a critical spirit,* and *an unbridled tongue* are three recognizable symptoms of weariness. God is concerned about our becoming weary because in this state we tend to revert back to our old nature and sinful behaviors. I am careful to guard against these things in my life, and I feel there is no excuse for holding on to sin since it can be easily detected and repented of.

Several years back, while laboring alongside my husband to plant what is now our local church, a guest speaker for our women's ministries came up to me and said, "I don't see rest in you!" Without fully knowing my situation, she began to instruct me, telling me to lay down my responsibilities. Her traveling companions joined in, and they implied that I was possessive and controlling. I was instructed to turn away from ministering to women for awhile and just care for myself.

Since I had expected to be encouraged, built up, and edified, this was a great blow to me. All I could do was sit there and weep. You see, I *was* tired, yet I loved what I was doing and it was what fulfilled me! I was comforted to a degree as our associate pastor's wife, Teri, came to my defense, but as she too began to weep from her own weariness, we both realized that we had a problem.

As I shared in Chapter 2, the Lord taught me to live by giving. And I believe in giving my life away. I believe in standing in the gap, in intercession for others, and I believe we are to engage in spiritual warfare, but I definitely didn't understand rest in the midst of all this! What these women were implying did not bear witness with either Teri or myself in our spirits, but we knew they did see something!

Suddenly, in the middle of their correction and instruction, the lead woman stopped the course of the conversation and apologized. Asking me to forgive her, she said that she felt she had been presumptuous and given a harsh word. The other women joined in apologizing, and we graciously accepted.

Even though it had been a painful experience for me, I told these women that I appreciated their insight. If this is what they perceived, then others might also. What grieved me the most was that I had been teaching about having a "meek and quiet spirit," but now, I felt that my life didn't display what I taught. As Teri and I drove away from that meeting, exhausted and wounded, *we vowed that we "would not rest" until we found out why we were weary*!

When I arrived home, I asked my husband if he felt that I had taken on more responsibilities than I should? What if he felt I had? I knew I would have to submit to his authority and that it would probably break my heart to lay these things down. It was God who had taken me out of myself and thrust me into serving His purposes, yet, I knew that I needed to confess my weariness and frustration to Jim and trust his leadership in my life.

Jim agreed that the women who had spoken these words to me were in error, but he strongly felt that God wanted to teach me something through this experience. Our associate pastor, Bill, responded to the suggestion of my laying down responsibilities by declaring, "Shirley, God has called you to more!"

After this, I tried everything I could think of to "chill out"! I tried taking naps. I read a book on jokes. I tried all types of activities to try to relax and lighten up. Finally, in desperation, I dropped down on my knees and cried out to the Lord to show me why I was weary in well doing.

In answer to my cry, God showed me a beautiful pastoral scene. The scene itself was a perfect picture of tranquillity. I saw grass was that was green, lush, and velvety, which surrounded a clean, still, crystal blue pond. The Shepherd was resting under a huge oak tree that cast a gentle shadow that gave shade to the many sheep resting along the water's bank. Some of the sheep were quietly lapping up water, while others grazed on the rich pasture. (See Psalm 23:1-6.)

One sheep nuzzled its head into the Shepherd's face, as if to express its love for Him. The Shepherd smiled and responded by affectionately scratching its ear. Next, the Shepherd pulled another sheep toward Him and began to treat its parasites. And another limped over to where the Shepherd sat so He could bind up its wounds.

In the background of this setting was a large mountain. Somehow I knew that the Shepherd and His flock would need to travel to cross over this mountain in a few days in order reach their next destination. Yet the entire scene was so beautiful and so restful that I can feel the peace of it even as I remember and write about it today.

Suddenly, the Lord turned my attention to one little lamb who was so excited about the next journey that it was enthusiastically hopping all around! God said, "Guess who that sheep is?!"

I immediately recognized that lamb as myself, and I began to feel a little embarrassed. The Lord then asked, "Do you ever feel like running while the Shepherd is pausing?" I confessed that I did, but what amazed me was that, as that little lamb, I had been completely oblivious to the call for rest and to the scene around me.

The Lord explained to me that He appreciates the zeal of His people. Their zeal is there because of their love for Him and His purposes, but often while they're running hard after Him, the enemy will fling out parasites and try to slow down their pace through sickness and disease. Some sheep are bitten by dogs. And even though the enthusiasm of these specially devoted sheep should motivate other sheep in their zeal to follow the Shepherd, sometimes it does the opposite! Jealousy will often cause one sheep to bite another sheep, while murmuring, "Who does she think she is?"

God doesn't want His children deceived into thinking that "loving not their lives unto death" means forsaking care and restoration from the Shepherd (see Rev. 12:11). *To restore* means to bring back to previous or original condition. Jesus is there to feed, guide, and shield us. He doesn't want us to lack and languish in need. Our Shepherd takes us to the fresh, tender, green pastures and to the still and restful waters. He *refreshes* our soul. To be refreshed means to be revived as with rest, food, drink, and to be stimulated! *Stimulate* means to rouse to activity or to increase action or interest.

No wonder I was weary in well doing. I wasn't in sin, rebellion, or prideful vanity. I was just so excited about the days ahead that I was neglecting the refreshing and restoring of my own soul. Then, when the Shepherd began to lead us to our next destination, I was more tired than the rest of the sheep because I had not rested as they had.

Through this, the Lord taught me to once again cast every care upon Him (see 1 Pet. 5:7). I realized that He affectionately cares for me and continually watches over me. In these times of restful companionship with the Shepherd, our soul is completely set upon Him and in Him (see Is. 26:3). Jesus is the One who sets our feet upon solid ground. It's not spiritual to neglect His care, it's foolish! God makes us strong and fit not only for the journey, but also for the battles ahead (see Ps. 16:8; 26:3).

Get Ready to Take the Land!

As we go, moving forward in wholeness to take hold of every part of the land our Father has for us, our purpose is not to just wander as before. Today, God is speaking to His Church as He did to Joshua, "Every place that the sole of

your foot shall tread upon, that have I given unto you..."
(Josh. 1:3). The Lord wants His daughters to take the land
that He has promised to us in our own lives, our families,
our cities, and the world.

When we walk in the presence and purposes of God, His
Kingdom is established, and the enemies of God quickly flee.
In Exodus, whenever the Ark of the Covenant was about to
move forward, Moses would say, "Rise up, Lord; let Your enemies be scattered; and let those who hate You flee before
You" (see Num. 10:35 AMP). Moses articulated these words,
but this time was only the beginning of victory for the children of Israel. Warfare with the enemy was still necessary for
them to take possession of the land of their inheritance.

We need to understand that this principle is still true
today. However, we don't wrestle against flesh and blood as
the Israelites did, but we are at war "...against principalities, against powers, against the rulers of the darkness of
this world, against spiritual wickedness in high places"
(Eph. 6:12). We must remember that God wants His people
to live in truth, holiness, and purity. He wants us to rely on
Him and be fully attuned to His plan and His purposes.
Simply being "ready" or "set" does not determine God's
timing to move forward. God will fulfill His purposes for
these last days through His people, but only those who will
walk *in* Him will be able to walk *with* Him (see Jn. 15:1-5).

In this hour, we need to get ready and get set so that we
might move aggressively forward as Christ's army and as
His ambassadors. Joshua 18:3 (AMP) says, "How long will
you be slack to go in and *possess the land* which the Lord,
the God of your fathers, has given you?" Likewise, the
apostle Paul appealed to the Ephesian church, begging them
to live in a way that would be a credit to their summons to
God's service:

*I therefore...beg you to walk (lead a life) worthy of
the [divine] calling to which you have been called...*
(Ephesians 4:1 AMP).

With God on our side, an exciting journey lies ahead.
Our Father has promised to go before us and to be with us
(see Deut. 31:8). There is no possible fulfillment on this
earth that is greater than to function as Daddy-God's representatives—taking back stolen ground, dispossessing enemies, and releasing prisoners to freedom in God's
Kingdom. A whole world awaits. God has so much for His
daughters, so let's prepare and take action to possess the
land for the glory of our Father and King and for His
Kingdom! Let us get ready now, get set now, and go...
where He goes!

Chapter 10

Women of Authority and Power

Yes, furthermore, I count everything as loss compared to the possession of the priceless privilege...of knowing Christ Jesus my Lord and of progressively becoming more deeply and intimately acquainted with Him [of perceiving and recognizing and understanding Him more fully and clearly]. For His sake I have lost everything and consider it all to be mere rubbish (refuse, dregs), in order that I may win (gain) Christ (the Anointed One), and that I may [actually] be found and known as in Him, not having any [self-achieved] righteousness that can be called my own, based on my obedience to the Law's demands (ritualistic uprightness and supposed right standing with God thus acquired), but posessing that [genuine righteousness] which comes through faith in Christ the Anointed One), the [truly] right standing with God, which comes from God by [saving] faith. [For my determined purpose is] that I may know Him [that I may progressively become more deeply and intimately acquainted with Him, perceiving and recognizing and understanding the wonders of His Person more strongly and more clearly], and that I may in that same way come to know the power outflowing from His resurrection [which it exerts over believers], and that I may so share His sufferings as to be continually transformed [in spirit into His likeness even] to His death... (Philippians 3:8-10 AMP).

The apostle Paul declared that his determined purpose was to intimately know Christ and the power overflowing from His resurrection that it exerts upon every believer. Within us is the potential to display God's glory as Christ did, but it can only be appropriated through intimacy with Him.

Become a Carrier of His Presence

God's presence is power, and wherever His power is manifested, He is present! Since God inhabits the praises of His people (see Ps. 22:3), we can expect His presence and power to be manifested whenever His people gather together in love, unity, and praise.

God's daughters have a destiny that is already laid out before them. Even though we may be "weaker vessels" than men (see 1 Pet. 3:7), awesome authority and power still belong to us as daughters of the King. Although a fine, porcelain cup is a fragile vessel in comparison to a bulky ceramic mug, it is still able to carry a comparable weight and volume of coffee or tea—no matter how hot it might be. Although fragile, God expects His daughters to be *carriers of His presence*!

"If Christ lives in us, controlling our personalities,
we will leave glorious marks on the lives we touch,
not because of us but because of him."
Eugenia Price

In the past, relatively few women have successfully rose to this purpose and call. Too many women have tried to promote themselves to positions of power or authority through an overbearing, manipulative, and usurping spirit. Women have tried to force open doors of opportunity through their own efforts and failed, creating fear and mistrust toward other women in the process.

At the same time, many of the King's precious, gifted daughters have remained standing in the background for too long. They have believed the lie that they couldn't possibly be powerful ambassadors and ministers in their Father's Kingdom. However, in this hour, God's Spirit is moving and motivating each of us as His daughters to arise and fulfill the royal role described for us in Proverbs 31. God is raising up His daughters to be women who are fully able and prepared to fulfill His mandate. He is calling us to be powerful women, who are strong in character and God-given ability.

God has not given us a spirit of timidity, but one of power, love, and a sound mind (see 2 Tim. 1:7). The Amplified Bible further explains that the mind Daddy-God has given is well-balanced, with discipline and self-control.

Love Takes First Place!

When Paul heard about the Colossian church's *love* in the Holy Spirit, he began to pray for them to also become filled with a deep and clear knowledge of God's will and purposes that they would live and conduct themselves in a manner worthy of the Lord. As he wrote in his Epistle to them:

> ...*Since the day we heard* [of your love in the Holy Spirit, we] *do not cease to pray for you, and to desire that ye might be filled with the knowledge of His will in all wisdom and spiritual understanding; that ye might walk worthy of the Lord unto all pleasing, being fruitful in every good work, and increasing in*

the knowledge of God; strengthened with all might, according to His glorious power, unto all patience and longsuffering with joyfulness; giving thanks unto the Father, which hath made us meet to be partakers of the inheritance of the saints in light (Colossians 1:9-11).

As I have emphasized throughout this book, God's top priority is love! It's who He is and what He is! It is God's love that chose us to be His very own children, even though we did not deserve it. It is His love that took Him to the cross, and it was the power of His love that raised Him from the dead. And now, by the power of His Spirit and His love, He works His own righteousness in and through us.

God is more interested in our character and spiritual condition than He is in putting on a show. God's spirit of power is given to us for the following reasons: first, to make us His own children; second, to be displayed in our life as we overcome sin and are brought to a place of maturity and effectiveness; third, that we might minister the power of the gospel with signs and wonders following.

A Holy Habitation of His Power and Presence

In these days, God is pouring out of His Spirit upon all flesh as was promised in His Word (see Joel 2:28-29). Great revivals are taking place all over the world. Now that people are waking out of their lethargy and slumber, God is beginning to come to visit His people. People are being saved, healed, and delivered from demonic bondage in greater and greater numbers. However, this is not the end of what God has purposed for His Church on the earth. He wants us to make ourselves ready to be a *holy habitation* of our God and King.

The time is coming when God's children will be carriers of His presence to such a degree that when Christians walk down a street, God's glory will descend upon the people around them. Conviction will fall upon simple bystanders.

Salvation, healing, and deliverance will become a common, daily occurrence. We will see headlines reading things like "Hospital Empties After Christians Walk In!" and "Thousands Healed and Converted to Jesus Christ at Local Coliseum." This is the Church that Jesus is coming back for!

As gross deception attempts to spread and fill this earth, greater grace from God will be seen and manifested than ever before in history. God's own power and authority have already been given to His sons and daughters, but the Spirit of the Lord will increase the degree of anointing to demonstrate this power and authority upon those who seek His face.

And all of us, as with an unveiled face, [because we] continued to behold [in the Word of God] as in a mirror the glory of the Lord, are constantly being transfigured into His very own image in ever increasing splendor and from one degree of glory to another; [for this comes] from the Lord [Who is] the Spirit (2 Corinthians 3:18 AMP).

If you walk in My statutes and keep My commandments and do them ... I will set My dwelling in and among you, and My soul shall not despise or reject or separate itself from you. And I will walk in and with and among you and will be your God, and you shall be My people (Leviticus 26:3,11-12 AMP).

Conditions for His Habitation

From the beginning of time, it has been God's intention to make His people His habitation. God promises His abiding presence; however, there are three requirements that we must fulfill in order to experience it in our lives.

1. God requires ongoing humility in our lives (see Jas. 4:6). Without humility, we won't even be able to touch the other requirements.

2. We need repentance, not simply that which brings salvation from eternal damnation, but that which expresses true sorrow for attitudes and behaviors that rise up and bring disgrace to the name that we bear. We must live the life of repentance that causes us to die daily (see 1 Cor. 15:31).

3. We must be truly hungry. When we are hungry, we are no longer satisfied by the delicious meal we had last Sunday. Instead, because of an ever-increasing hunger, we say, "Mmmm-mm! That was good, I want more!" (see Ps. 34:8) Matthew 5:6 says, "Blessed are they which do hunger and thirst after righteousness: for they shall be filled."

Don't Stop—Press On!

Throughout the centuries, we see a pattern of God's people going "just so far" in seeking after Him, then stopping. In my own life, I have times in which my walk with God was intimate and wonderful, and then, suddenly, something happened that caused that closeness to cease. God doesn't want halfhearted seeking or temporary relationships with His daughters. In Jeremiah 29:13-14 (AMP), He promises, "Then you will seek Me...and find Me when you search for Me with all your heart. I will be found of you, says the Lord, and I will release you from captivity and gather you...."

Why do we forget humility? Why do we become satisfied and walk in our own way? We must consider who we are when nobody is watching. In our private times and personal thoughts, is our heart right before Him? God is looking for a people whose hearts are pure, upright, and honest before Him. If we ask God for wisdom to walk after Him, He will give it to us (see Jas. 1:5). In fact, God's purpose for the Church is found in Ephesians 3:10:

To the intent that now unto the principalities and powers in heavenly places might be known by the church the manifold wisdom of God.

This verse tells us that the Church will make known the "many sided" wisdom of God to principalities, powers, and rulers of darkness! As we make His wisdom known to the enemies of God, we will move in a high realm of authority and power!

I sought God as to why I often repeated the pattern of going "just so far" in intimacy with Him and then stopping. In answer, He showed me the key that would open the door that often seemed to block the continual progress in our relationship.

The Lord showed me a picture of how He loves His people, touching and embracing us with His goodness and grace in many ways. He takes away the rags that we've worn, burns them, and replaces them with rich linens and robes. I saw how God calls us to Himself and loves us. Then, I saw God take a step backward and upward; He stood back, watching and waiting. He wanted to see if we would press in toward Him, desiring to be changed more into His image and go another degree higher into His presence and glory or would we just stand there frustrated and complaining that although we couldn't quite put our finger on what it was, things just weren't the same. With this latter mentality, we become distracted and begin to step back from Him ourselves.

In marriage, a lot of couples experience sweet romance, intense love, and then boredom. Sometimes, when boredom sets in, one or even both parties might become distracted and commit adultery. This has been a terrible fact, even among Christians. However, to experience sweet romance and intense love once again, one must start appreciating and loving again. It's a choice. As we press in to know, understand, and love someone, our love will continue to grow.

Guard the Faithfulness of Your Heart

The Lord spoke to me, saying, "Warn My daughters against spiritual adultery!" As I thought upon what He had said, He continued: "In the natural, if a man even looks upon a woman and lusts in his heart, he's already committed adultery (see Mt. 5:28). After testing My people to see if they will press into Me so that they might come higher into My presence, they have looked away instead of seeking My face. When they begin to flirt with selfishness, pride, anger, and the other things that I have so mercifully removed from their lives, they have committed adultery already!"

This is why it's so important to walk in repentance every day; it's the gateway to deliverance! If we want to walk in authority and power as God's daughters, we must go higher with Him and continually be changed from one degree of glory to the next (see 2 Cor. 3:18). If we want more of God and if we want to carry His anointing, *we must compromise less*. This does not include just when we're being watched by others, but also when we are alone. God sees each heart and the desires and intentions that it holds.

When we aren't pressing into God, our attitude will always show it, and when we aren't walking in the Spirit, we *will* fulfill the lusts of the flesh. Christians often wonder why they stumble and sin, but God told me, "The sins of the flesh is only the fruit of sin against God." That's why King David, after he compromised and sinned in committing adultery and murder, said, "Against You, and You alone have I sinned!" (See Psalm 51:4.) He wasn't establishing a biblical principle that excluded accountability or confession of our faults to one another, but he was saying that his sin was the fruit of losing his passion for God. It's so simple! As long as David fervently loved and worshiped God, he was able to walk uprightly before Him.

Leviticus 26:3,11-12, which we looked at previously, tells us that if we keep God's commandments, then He will dwell in and among us and we will be His holy habitation. This requirement sounds impossible, for we might easily slip up on one of God's many commandments. However, Matthew 22:37-40 shows us what fulfills the entire law:

> ...*Thou shalt love the Lord thy God with all thy heart, and with all thy soul, and with all thy mind. This is the first and great commandment. And the second is like unto it, thou shalt love thy neighbour as thyself. On these two commandments hang all the law and the prophets.*

We must first and foremost love the Lord our God with every part of our being. As we love Him with all our heart, soul, mind, and strength, our mouth will speak forth that love out of our heart (see Mt. 12:34-35). Our life (which is expressed through our emotions and personality) will demonstrate His love. The comprehension of His wonderful and mysterious ways will be unfolded and expressed through us, and all of our efforts in life will be for His glory!

Abiding Love Is Fruitful

All God really wants from us is our love. In the revival that's taking place around the world, people are giving testimonies of falling in love with the Lord like they never imagined they could. Jesus taught us about the relationship between love and God's abiding presence:

> *If ye love Me, keep My commandments. ... He that hath My commandments, and keepeth them, he it is that loveth Me: and he that loveth Me shall be loved of My Father, and I will love him, and will manifest Myself to him. ...If a man love me, he will keep My words: and My Father will love him, and We will*

come unto him, and make Our abode with him (John 14:15,21,23).

Abide in Me, and I in you. As the branch cannot bear fruit of itself, except it abide in the vine; no more can ye, except ye abide in Me. I am the vine, ye are the branches: He that abideth in Me, and I in him, the same bringeth forth much fruit: for without Me ye can do nothing (John 15:4-5).

Herein is My Father glorified, that ye bear much fruit; so shall ye be My disciples ... Ye have not chosen Me, but I have chosen you, and ordained you, that ye should go and bring forth fruit, and that your fruit should remain: that whatsoever ye shall ask of the Father in My name, He may give it you (John 15:8,16).

If we love God, we will obey Him. He will reveal and manifest Himself to us, and He will make His abode with us. If we will dwell in God, He will dwell in us and we will show ourselves to be His true followers. We will bear much fruit and whatever we ask will be done when we dwell in Him and He dwells in us!

Psalm 91 tells us that we will remain stable when we make the Lord God our dwelling place. Our Father will deliver us from the snare of the enemy. We will not be afraid, and no evil will befall us. Because God is our dwelling place, He will give His angels charge over us, and we will trample our enemies under our feet! This sounds to me like authority and power is given to those who abide in God.

Psalm 91:14-15 (AMP) tells us why this authority and power is given to a daughter or son of God who abides in Him:

*Because he has set his **love** upon Me...because he knows and understands My name [has a personal knowledge of My mercy, love, and kindness—trusts and relies on Me, knowing I will never forsake him,*

*no, never]. He shall call upon Me, and I will answer
him, I will be with him in trouble, and I will deliver
him and honor him.*

A people without passion is a people without purpose.
Today, God is restoring His passion through revival. A passionate Church will desire to be a pure and holy Bride for
her Beloved. A passionate Church cannot and will not be
lukewarm; it will be aflame for its God. A passionate people are ready and waiting to do God's will because love is
active, not passive.

It's time to get the house clean, individually and as a corporate Body, because the Master's coming. Now is the time
to prepare. We must stop shoving things in corners and saying, "I'll get to that later." Uncompromising order will be
necessary to make ready a holy habitation for God's abiding presence. God is about to come to His Church in all His
splendor, glory, and power to display His wonderful brilliance to a world in desperate need of Light.

*Your testimonies are very sure; holiness [apparent in
separation from sin, with simple trust and hearty obedience] is becoming to Your house O Lord, forever*
(Psalm 93:5 AMP).

The Bread That Satisfies

In John chapter 6, Jesus fed the multitude of 5,000 people
with five barley loaves and two fish, and there were several
baskets of leftovers. God is not only able to miraculously provide all that we need, but He is able to give us far more than
we need.

After Jesus tremendously blessed the people with this
miraculous provision, the Scripture says that He withdrew
Himself to be alone (see Jn. 6:15). The disciples then got
into their boats, and when He had not returned by nightfall,
they began to sail across the sea toward Capernaum. When

Jesus came back, the boat was gone, so Jesus walked across the sea to join them. The next day, when the followers realized that the disciples' boat had departed and Jesus wasn't among them, they also got into their boats and crossed the sea *looking for Jesus* (see Jn. 6:22-24).

With today's revival, there seems to be leftovers every time God feeds and blesses His people. As we experience His tangible presence, along with the miraculous, I believe that His intention is for us to press in and say, "More!" He wants us to follow Him, and to cross over to the next place where He is going.

When the people found Jesus, He said to them, "I assure you, most solemnly I tell you, you have been searching for Me, not because you saw the miracles and signs, but because you were fed with the loaves and were filled and satisfied!" (Jn. 6:26 AMP)

The people then asked for a sign or miracle like bread from Heaven, such as their forefathers had eaten in the wilderness. However, Jesus told them,

> ...*Verily, verily, I say unto you, Moses gave you not that bread from heaven; but My Father giveth you the true bread from heaven. For the bread of God is He which cometh down from heaven, and giveth life unto the world. ...I am the bread of life: he that cometh to Me shall never hunger; and he that believeth on Me shall never thirst* (John 6:32-33,35).

Jesus told them that the bread God had rained from Heaven for Moses wasn't really the Bread from Heaven. It was merely a "type" of the Bread from Heaven, and it needed to be partaken of daily, but Jesus said, "I am the Bread from Heaven!"

If we want to be filled with God's presence and move in His authority and power as He has called us to do, we must partake of *Him* daily. Some of God's daughters need to learn how to eat again, for they have become anorexic and bulimic. They haven't taken in enough of the Word of God, nor have they kept down what they have received from Him. Instead, they have regurgitated what they've eaten. If we go too long without eating food, we'll lose our appetite, so sometimes we need to make ourselves sit down and eat.

If it's been a while since you've partaken of the Lord, I suggest starting with a little sliver of Bread. Then come back for another sliver...then a thin slice, a fat chunk, and finally, the whole Loaf! After that, you'll feel as if you can't get enough. That's okay, though, you need never worry about running out, for there's *plenty of Bread*, enough for eternity!

A friend of mine, Carol Mast, once said, "God is very accommodating. If all we want is a crumb, He'll give us a crumb. However, if we want the whole Loaf, there's always fresh Bread for God's Children. He will give us as much as we want!"

God wants us to taste and see that He is *good* (see Ps. 34:8). Jesus said, "Blessed...are you who hunger and seek with eager desire now, for you shall be filled and completely satisfied!" (Lk. 6:21a)

After Moses approached the Lord telling Him that even though God had already delivered the people out of bondage, parted the Red Sea, destroyed their enemies, led them with a cloud by day and a pillar of fire by night, the people were now irritated because God hadn't given them bread. God had never planned on starving them. But, perhaps all He wanted was for the people to look to Him and ask.

God said, "...Behold, I will rain bread from heaven for you; and the people shall go out and gather a day's portion every day, that I may prove them, whether they will walk in My law, or not" (Ex. 16:4 AMP).

Remember, the sum of God's law is loving Him. We'll do everything He requires us to do if we truly love God; our words and actions will be an expression of our heart. Today, God is feeding us because He wants us to be filled, full, satisfied, and then hungry again for more of Him, but I also believe He is "proving," or testing, us to see if we will walk in His love. If we will, we will be completely devoted to Him—for better, for worse; for richer, for poorer; in sickness and in health; forever!

"We are called to be God's transmitters, to be completely separated from all thoughts which are contrary to his thinking, so that we may transmit his thoughts to others."
Hannah Hurnard

Only as we become filled with God can we know the power of the resurrection. The same power that raised Jesus from the dead, lives within us! It is at work to perfect and transform us into the image of our Father and do to in and through us far above what we have ever before dreamed:

Now to Him Who, by (in consequence of) the [action of His] power that is at work within us, is able to [carry out His purpose and] do super-abundantly, far over and above all that we [dare] to ask or think, [infinitely beyond our highest prayers, desires, thoughts, hopes, or dreams] (Ephesians 3:20 AMP).

Robert Smith, a new convert in our church, read about Abraham asking God if He would spare the city of Sodom from destruction if there were ten righteous persons in the land (see Gen. 18). As a result, this new convert decided to ask the Lord if He was able pick out 30 righteous persons at the factory where he was employed. When the Lord told him, "No," Robert asked if He could pick out 20, then 10. After telling Robert "No" each time, God finally told him,

"But you can pick out as many as you want, and I can save them all!"

When we really realize that the power of the resurrection is at work in and through every believer, nothing will hold us back. And united together in love and devotion, we cannot fail. We will turn the world upside down!

After being amazed by the accuracy of a word of knowledge that I had given someone several years ago, I looked up toward Heaven and asked, "How did I do that?"

God responded, "You in Me, and Me in you, is powerful!" Then He continued, "...But My people united in Me, and Me in them...you can't even begin to imagine the power!" God's daughters are a part of His people, and He is waiting for us to arise and function as a part of His royal nation!

Arise, Beautiful Warrior!

A few years ago, several women from our church gathered every Friday afternoon at a local park. Our children would eat and play together while we prayed for revival to come to our city. One Friday while we were praying, the Lord gave me a vision of His daughters filled and moving with authority and power.

I saw tremendous warfare going on in the city. All the godly men that we knew were in the heat of the battle along the front line. Satan and his forces were trying to press in against them, but they could not prevail. Warfare continued on and on. Then, suddenly, women began to appear in the background. These women were wearing the most beautiful, stunning, and dazzling gowns I had ever seen. While I marveled at their radiance, the Lord spoke to me and said, "These are their battle garments!"

God had not clothed His daughters for battle with ugly, green army fatigues; these beautiful gowns represented the beauty of holiness and the righteousness of God upon their lives.

As the women drew near to the front line, the men turned and watched them approach the battle. Because the women's gowns were perfect—without any marks of jealousy, competition, manipulation, or usurpation—the men quickly extended their arms toward each woman and motioned for them to take the places and positions alongside them.

The looks on their faces showed that these men had been waiting a long time for the women to come. Not one of the men looked at them and said, "Women, you're out of place, who do you think you are?" Instead, they placed them in positions of power and authority right by their sides!

The most thrilling part of this vision is how I saw satan respond. When he saw the women coming, he grabbed his head with both hands, pulled his hair as if he might go insane, and doubled over, screaming, "Oh, no! Here they come again!" Then, when he saw the men give the women their rightful place, he turned and fled!

Satan didn't flee because he thinks women are more powerful in spirit than men, but because he knows that when the Church (which consists of both sons and daughters) comes together to function properly in love and unity, nothing can withstand its power or the blessings that our Father commands!

We live in such an exciting time. We truly have been brought into the Kingdom "for such a time as this"! (See Esther 4:14.) If we will simply embrace the truth of God's purpose for our lives and act upon it in humility and obedience, we will experience power and victory in every area of our lives!

Know What Is Yours!

The Lord often speaks to my heart through simple and humorous situations. The other day while I was reading and enjoying the sunshine on my deck, the Lord spoke to my heart again about arising as women of authority and women of power.

Most of my neighbors were off at work, and there was little sound but that of the birds singing and chirping in the air. Suddenly, I heard a loud, strong buzz! The sound wasn't moving around; it was clearly isolated and coming from not far away. I looked to see what was making the noise, and I saw a huge bumble bee hovering about three feet from my chair. It was completely still other than its wings that were buzzing in the air, and it was pointed right at me as if it were in "attack" position! I know this sounds funny, but I'm almost positive that I could see its eyes—and they were seriously warning me to move from where I was at!

My lounge chair on the deck had a cushion on it with large, beautiful flowers printed all over it, and I occupied that seat! Anyway, I quickly moved. As I did, it charged toward me. It quickly circled around me twice, as if to say, "Good thinking...and don't come back!"

Well, I did go back—because it was my chair!

The Lord showed me two things from this amusing incident. First, He showed me how funny, silly, and pathetic we must look to ministering angels (whom our Father has sent to war on our behalf) every time we give up our rightful place in His Kingdom. Too often we allow ourselves to be intimidated by the sound of satan's threats and back away from what we are doing, relinquishing our position. Second, my Father made me realize that *we* need to become like that bee in the sense that He has also given us a sound. Our mighty sound is the sound of joy, praise, and war! It truly is a sound that terrifies and intimidates the enemy, and it is very effective.

Satan has been stealing the beautiful things that God has given to us for far too long. It's time that we take the offensive position, look him right in the eyes, and let him know that we are taking back what is rightfully ours. Our Father has already given us both the authority and power we need to do so!

A Prayer for God's Daughters

Father, we are privileged to be among Your honorable women. As Your daughters, we seek You for purpose and fulfillment! May we be filled with the deep and clear knowledge of Your will, and may we have comprehensive insight into Your ways and purposes. Grant us understanding and discernment of spiritual things so that we might live and conduct ourselves in a manner that is worthy of You!

Father, may we be pleasing to You in all things, and may we bear fruit in every good work, steadily growing and increasing in and by Your knowledge as we grow in deeper, clearer insight and recognition of Your ways and Your purposes.

Finally, we pray that we might be invigorated and strengthened with all power according to the might of Your glory, that we might exercise every kind of endurance and patience with joy.

God, You are our strength, our personal bravery, and our invincible army; You make our feet firm and steady in rough places in the face of every circumstance. You help us to make spiritual progress in each area of our lives as we seek and submit ourselves to You.

Thank You! We love You, Daddy-God!

For more information regarding speaking engagements for Shirley Sustar, you may contact Shirley through the following:

Mail:	6294 Hoffman Road
	Wooster, OH 44691
Phone:	(330) 345-6780
E-mail:	JRSUSTAR@aol.com

Exciting titles

by Debby Jones and Jackie Kendall

LADY IN WAITING
by Debby Jones and Jackie Kendall.
This is not just another book for singles! With humor, honesty, and biblical truths, the authors help point women to *being* the right woman and not just finding the right man! With *Lady in Waiting*, any woman—married or single—will learn that only a relationship with Jesus will satisfy!
ISBN 1-56043-848-7 $9.99p

LADY IN WAITING Devotional Journal & Study Guide
by Debby Jones and Jackie Kendall.
You can keep the principles taught in *Lady in Waiting* in your heart by learning to apply them with this devotional journal and study guide. These questions, quotes, thoughts, and teachings will help you to become the woman of God that He designed you to be. You also can record your spiritual growth in a specially designed journal section. Don't miss this opportunity to become God's "Lady in Waiting"!
ISBN 1-56043-298-5 $7.99p

LUNATIC ON A LIMB WITH JESUS
by Jackie Kendall.
Do you ever feel like life has you dangling from a tree limb? Don't worry! You can survive—just look up to Jesus! Take one day at a time with this humorous, autobiographical devotional by the irrepressible Jackie Kendall. Discover how you can survive life's surprises and come out smiling!
ISBN 1-56043-306-X $9.99p

HOW TO AVOID A BOZO—*NEW VIDEO!*
Help for Finding God's Best in a Mate
by Jackie Kendall.
Do you want to find God's best—Mr. Right? Learn the differences between a man worth waiting for and a Bozo. Don't let your lover be a loser!
1 video ISBN 0-7684-0070-8 Retail $14.99

Available at your local Christian bookstore.

Internet: http://www.reapernet.com